Kabbalah
for Beginners

Kabbalah
for Beginners

4th Edition

LAITMAN
KABBALAH PUBLISHERS

Rav Michael Laitman, PhD

KABBALAH FOR BEGINNERS

Published by Laitman Kabbalah Publishers
www.kabbalah.info   info@kabbalah.info
1057 Steeles Avenue West, Suite 532, Toronto, ON, M2R 3X1, Canada
194 Quentin Rd, 2nd floor, Brooklyn, New York, 11223, USA

Printed in Canada

Library of Congress Cataloging-in-Publication Data
Laitman, Michael.
Kabbalah for beginners / Michael Laitman. — 4th ed.
p. cm.
ISBN 978-0-9781590-9-2
1. Cabala. I. Title.
BM525.L252 2007
296.1'6–dc22   2007021769

Research: Eli Vinokur, Oren Levi
Photos: Moshe Admoni
Layout: Richard Aquan
Graphics: Baruch Khovov
Copy Editor: Claire Gerus
Printing and Post Production: Uri Laitman
Executive Editor: Chaim Ratz

FOURTH EDITION: OCTOBER 2007
First printing

KABBALAH FOR BEGINNERS

TABLE OF CONTENTS

INTRODUCTION

Scientists have been studying the laws of Nature, our be-havior, and our place in the world for thousands of years. Yet, these days, scientists are realizing that the more they advance in their research, the more confusing they find the world to be.

While science has undoubtedly brought enormous progress to our lives, there are boundaries beyond which it cannot penetrate. For instance, scientific tools cannot measure the human soul, or the basic motivation for our actions. If it could, we would be able to "program" people to behave as we wish. But because we cannot perceive our most essential motivations, we humans, the apex of Cre-ation, are still unaware of why we come into this world!

Man has always been searching for the answers to life's most basic questions: "Who am I?" "What is the purpose of my life?" "Why does the world exist?" "Do we continue to exist after our physical being has ended?"

In the absence of sufficient answers, some find temporary refuge in Eastern teachings, meditations, or techniques that minimize personal expectations and reduce the suffering caused by disillusionment.

However, experience teaches us that we can never satisfy all our desires; therefore, we will always experience some degree of discontentment. Yet, at the deepest level of our being, the true basis for suffering arises from our inability to answer life's most fundamental question: "Why am I here?"

Kabbalah answers this very question, and in doing so, guides us toward complete and lasting satisfaction. It teaches us how to access the essential feeling of the spiritual realm—the sixth sense—and thus improve our lives in this world. With it, we can perceive the Upper World—the Creator—and assume control over our lives.

The Bible, *The Book of Zohar*, *The Tree of Life*, *The Study of the Ten Sefirot*, and other authentic Kabbalistic sources were given to us to promote us in the spiritual realms. With their help, we can obtain spiritual knowledge. They explain how we can turn our lives in this world into a path to spiritual ascent.

Over the generations, Kabbalists have written many books in various styles, each adapted to the era in which they lived. Similarly, *Kabbalah for Beginners* has been written to help you take your first steps towards understanding the roots of human behavior and the laws of Nature. The contents present the essential principles of the wisdom of Kabbalah and describe how these principles work. This book is intended for those searching for a reliable method of studying our world. It is written for those seeking to understand the reasons for suffering and pleasure, who strive to take charge over their lives and make them the exciting and joyous journeys they can be.

* This book is based on essays and lectures given by Rav Michael Laitman, PhD, which were then edited by staff members of the Ashlag Research Institute (ARI).

PART ONE

The History
of Kabbalah

There is no real difference between the history of Kabbalah and the history of the world, except that Kabbalah tells the same story from the spiritual perspective. It is similar to examining our lives from two very different perspectives. From the historical perspective, our past is a sequence of events that happened to us or to our ancestors, while from the Kabbalistic perspective, our past is a sequence of spiritual events, expressed in a series of scenes we call "life on Earth."

As we will see in Part Three, history isn't really "unfolding" in Kabbalah; rather, it is experienced within each and every one of us separately. Kabbalists don't relate to the external reality as a tangible reality, but explain that what we perceive as "external" is really a reflection of images that exist only within us.

Part One of the book will discuss the history of Kabbalah as experiences that occurred in the physical world. Part Two will explore the origin and structure of reality. Part Three will examine our inner reality, and Part Four combines all three into one coherent, practical worldview.

1
KABBALAH CHRONICLES

The Rambam (Maimonides), a great 12th century Kabbalist, wrote that thousands of years ago, when humanity was deep in idol worship, one man couldn't go with the flow. His name was Abraham, and today we know him as "Abraham the Patriarch." Abraham pondered and searched until he found the truth: that the world had only *one* leader.

When he discovered this, he realized he had uncovered life's eternal truth, and ran to share it with the world. To clarify his message, he developed a method that helped him explain his perceptions more clearly. Since then, the world has had a method that reveals this truth. Today this method is as valid as it was then, and we call it "the wisdom of Kabbalah."

STAGE ONE

In Chapter One of his book, *The Mighty Hand*, Maimonides describes how there was a time when people knew that there was only one force governing the world. He explained that after some time, due to a prolonged spiritual decline, they all forgot it. Instead, people believed that there were many forces in the world, each with its own responsibilities. Some forces were responsible for food provision, some were meant to help us marry more successfully, and some were in charge of keeping us wealthy and healthy.

But one man, whom we now know as Abraham, noticed that all these forces obeyed the same rules of birth and death, budding and withering. To discover what those rules were, he began to study Nature. Abraham's research taught him that there was really only one force, and everything else was only a partial manifestation of it. This was Stage One of the spiritual evolution of humanity.

Perhaps one of the best known Native American traditions is the Council Circle. Here, the members sit in a circle, each member expressing a different aspect of the same issue. Similarly, Abraham didn't want to see things only from his perspective. He wanted to see through everyone's eyes, and thus discover the one force that made different people see different things.

Once Abraham discovered this truth, he began to spread the word. Challenged by having to explain a concept that contradicted everything his contemporaries believed, Abraham was forced to develop a teaching method that would help him reveal this concept to them. This was the prototype of the teaching method we now call "Kabbalah" (from the Hebrew word, *Lekabel*, to receive). Today, Kabbalah teaches us how to discover the force that guides us, and in doing so, receive infinite joy and pleasure.

We will talk about Abraham's discovery in greater detail later in the book, but we should mention here that the essence of his discovery is that the universe is "obeying" a force of love and giving. This force is what Abraham and all the prophets in the Bible call "The Creator." When Biblical figures speak of the Creator, or the Lord, or God, they speak not of a being, but of a force of love and giving, and how they perceive it. If we keep this in mind, we will find the method of Kabbalah very clear and easy to understand.

Abraham's discovery was no coincidence. It arrived just in time to counter an outbreak of egoism and selfishness that threatened to destroy both the love and unity among people, and between humankind and the Creator.

This unity was the natural way of life for humanity prior to the time of the Tower of Babel. This is what the Bible means by, "And the whole earth was of one language and of one speech" (Genesis 11:1). Everyone knew about the Creator, the force of love and giving, and all were united with it. People experienced it as part of their lives, and they didn't need to "work" on their unity, as is done today, because no egoism was setting them apart.

This is why the Bible writes that they were of "one language" and "one speech."

But as soon as people's egoism began to develop, they wanted to use their unity for their own benefit. This prompted the Creator's concern. Put differently, the force of love had to act to counter humankind's egoism-caused separation. In the words of Genesis, "The Lord said, 'Behold, they are one people, and they all have the same language. ...and now nothing which they purpose to do will be impossible for them'" (Genesis 11:6).

To save humanity from its own egoism, the Creator, the single force discovered by Abraham, could do one of two things: disperse humanity and thus prevent a catastrophic clash of self-interests, or teach people how to overcome their egoism.

The latter option offered an obvious benefit: if people remained united despite their egoism, they would not only retain their way of life, they would actually unite even more closely with the Creator. In other words, the efforts to bond, despite their growing egoism, would force people to become much more aligned and united with both the Creator and each other.

Here's an illustration of this principle: Imagine you are rich and want a shiny new Jaguar. This is no big deal; you just walk into the nearest dealership and come out driving the car of your dreams. How long do you think your pleasure would last? A week? Probably even less. And how much would you really care about your new

Jag, which demanded nothing more than a visit to the dealership to get it?

But if you were *not* well off and had to work two shifts for two whole years to get that Jaguar, you would undoubtedly love and appreciate your car very much. The effort you put into "attaching" yourself to it would make that car much more important to you.

This is the benefit of bonding with the Creator despite growing egoism. Egoism serves an important purpose: it is there to give you something to strive to overcome, a "practice field" where you can make efforts that will make you appreciate the force of love—the Creator.

(Abraham thought): "'How is it possible that this wheel will always steer without a driver? And who is driving it? After all, it cannot drive itself!' And he had no teacher, and no one to let him know. Instead, he was... surrounded by idolaters, fools. And his father and his mother, and all the people were idolaters. And he, too, was idol worshipping with them. And his heart roamed and understood, until he attained the path of truth."

--Maimonides, *Yad HaChazakah (The Mighty Hand)*, Idolatry Rules

---

So the Creator revealed Himself to Abraham to show him how humanity could "practice" and "work" at loving the Creator, and thus become closer to Him. This is also why Abraham was such an enthusiastic disseminator of his method. He knew that time was of the essence: either he taught his people how to unite through bonding with the Creator—the force of love—or their growing egoism would alienate them from one another and they would disperse or kill each other off.

As the Bible and other ancient Hebrew texts teach us, the Babylonians rejected and scorned Abraham's offer. Abraham confronted their king, Nimrod, and proved that his method could work. But instead of adopting it, Nimrod attempted to assassinate Abraham. Now, with his life at stake, Abraham fled from Babylon and began to teach his method while roaming "from town to town and from kingdom to kingdom, until he arrived in the Land of Israel" (Maimonides, *The Mighty Hand*, Idolatry Rules, Chapter 1).

Despite hardships and challenges, Abraham's teachings gained some support, and his followers helped him share his knowledge with others, filling the ranks with "new recruits." In time, the lone fighter for truth had multiplied, creating a nation whose name, "the nation of Israel," symbolizes the one thing they had in common—their desire for the Creator. The word "Israel" is really a combination of two Hebrew words: *Yashar* (straight) and *El* (God). The people of Israel are those who have one desire in their hearts: to be like the Creator, united by altruism and love.

The collapse of the Tower of Babel was not, however, the end of the story, but only the beginning. The force of love, which Abraham had discovered, wanted to tighten its bond with humanity. But since the Creator is a force of love, and loves us as much as anyone can love another, the only tightening of the bond can come from us. Hence, this force, the Creator, keeps increasing our egoism, so we may rise above it by strengthening our ties with Him.

For those who want to remain egoists, increased egoism means greater alienation. As a result, the people who were once united split into different nations and invented new technologies with which they could create new weapons. They used these weapons to protect what they thought was their freedom, but which was actually their increased self-centeredness and alienation from the Creator and from one another.

Without noticing it, they became increasingly subjugated to their egoism while mistakenly thinking they were defending themselves from those who wanted to harm them. Their egoism made them forget that when they were united, they hadn't needed weapons, as they had no egoism to make them feel their freedom was threatened.

But those who wanted to remain united, and even deepen their bond of love, treated their increased egoism as an opportunity for growth. To them, it was a welcome challenge, rather than a problem or crisis.

But to cope with their heightened egoism they needed to upgrade Abraham's method. This was Moses' cue. As with the Babylonians and their king, Nimrod, overcoming the new level of egoism—this time represented by the Egyptians and their king, Pharaoh—meant escaping it.

Pharaoh wasn't simply an evil king. He actually brought Israel (those who want the Creator) closer to the Creator. In Kabbalah, Pharaoh is the epitome of egoism, and the only way to escape him is to unite (with each other and with the Creator). As we've seen before, unity makes you closer (more similar) to the Creator. To defeat Pharaoh, Moses returned to Egypt after his escape, united the people around the same idea that Abraham promoted many years previously, and once again helped his people escape.

But this time, Israel defeated a much more powerful ego. Pharaoh was not like Nimrod, King of Babel; he could not be defeated by one determined man. Defeating Pharaoh required a whole, united nation. And because Moses needed to teach Abraham's method to a whole nation, he wrote a new book, an adaptation of Abraham's teachings for an entire nation: The Torah (Pentateuch).

But the Creator, being a force of love and generosity, wanted to give more than to just one nation. He wanted the *whole world* to know that there was only one force and that they would take the gift He wished to give humanity—Himself.

So while Moses' Torah was a big step forward, since it helped a whole nation connect with the Creator, it was not the end of the road. The end of the road will arrive only when the whole world is in touch with Him, experiencing the bond of love and unity that the ancient Babylonians did, before the first outbreak of egoism. Put differently, the end of the road will arrive when all of humanity reclaims what it once had, and then lost.

In the article, "The Essence of the Wisdom of Kabbalah," Kabbalist Rabbi Yehuda Ashlag describes the purpose of Creation as a "single, exalted goal described as 'the revelation of His Godliness to His creatures in this world.'"

STAGE TWO

The second stage in humanity's spiritual evolution started about two thousand years ago, when *The Book of Zohar*, the most important book of Kabbalah, was written and then concealed. It was written shortly after the people of Israel were exiled for what was to be their last and longest exile.

Just like Abraham and Moses in Stage One, the second stage had two giants of its own: Rabbi Shimon Bar-Yochai (Rashbi) and The Holy Ari (Rabbi Isaac Luria). Rashbi's *Book of Zohar* is, as the book itself states, a commentary on the Torah. Just as Moses explained Abraham's words to the entire nation, *The Book of Zohar* is intended to explain Moses' words to the entire world. This is why one often reads that *The Book of Zohar* is destined to appear in the time of the Messiah, at the "end of days." It is also why Rabbi Yehuda Ashlag, the great twentieth-century Kabbalist, wrote that the rediscovery of *The Book of Zohar* is proof that the "days of the Messiah" are here.

As always, the only antidote to a rise in egoism is unity, and the greater the egoism, the more important it is for people to unite. At first, uniting Abraham's followers and family was enough. Then, when Moses fled from Egypt, he had to unite a whole nation in order to succeed. Today, we need to unite the whole of humanity. Egoism has reached such intensity that unless the whole of humankind unites to overcome it, we will not succeed.

"I have found it written that the above decree to not openly engage in the wisdom of truth was only for a time—until the end of 1490. From then on ...the sentence has been lifted, and permission has been given to engage in *The Book of Zohar*. And from the year 1540 it has become praiseworthy to engage in great numbers, since it is by this virtue that the Messiah King will come, and not by another virtue."

-- Rabbi Avraham Azulai
Introduction to the book, *Ohr ha Chama (Light of the Sun)*

The second stage in the process of humanity's bonding with the Creator was very different from the first. It was a time of subtle growth, when the tool to unite humanity—the wisdom of Kabbalah—was being refined and improved in dimly lit rooms and within small, inconspicuous groups. This is why the two most significant works of that period, Rashbi's *Book of Zohar* and the Ari's *Tree of Life*, were hidden by their own authors as soon as they were completed. They resurfaced many years later, and in the case of *The Zohar*, many centuries later.

STAGE THREE

The third and last stage of humanity's spiritual evolution began in the 1990s. In 1945, Rabbi Yehuda Ashlag, author of the *Sulam* (Ladder) commentary on *The Book of Zohar*, predicted that the final stage would begin in 1995. Similarly, the Vilna Gaon (GRA) wrote in his book, *The Voice of the Turtledove*, that this stage would begin in 1990. Many other Kabbalists made similar predictions, leading to the conclusion that the future is already here, and now is the time to unite as one and defeat egoism once and for all.

Humanity's entire history is paved with battles against egoism, followed by attempts to unite despite it. Today, most scientists agree that man's self-centeredness and misunderstanding of Nature's rules are the causes of all that is wrong with our world. Yehuda Ashlag wrote about this in the 1930s and 1940s, but in those days, he was a voice in the wilderness.

In recent years it has become evident that unless we change ourselves, the world will not change for the better. In fact, we are ruining our planet and our society in so many ways that solving the problems separately has become impossible. To solve our problems, we need an inclusive solution, which can only be found when we transform human egoism into altruism, and bond with the force of love—the Creator.

In his article, "Peace in the World," Ashlag writes that if we unite, every single member of humankind will personally experience the Creator in the deepest sense of the word, as it is written, "they shall all know Me, from the least of them unto the greatest of them" (Jeremiah 31:33). The wisdom of Kabbalah has been prepared as a method that can help us do just that—unite—and experience the Creator. In his "Introduction to the Book of Zohar," Ashlag wrote that if we integrate Kabbalah into our day-to-day lives, we will achieve the goal for which we were created, and we will again be "of one language and of one speech," at one with the Creator, and we will never to part again.

2
TIMELESS TEACHERS OF KABBALAH

Through the ages, many Kabbalists have written profound and beautiful books. But we would like to focus on four very special Kabbalists and their books. These men wrote their books specifically to help beginners become acquainted with Kabbalah. The exception is Rabbi Akiva, who did not leave a book as his contribution. Instead, he gifted us with such convincing concepts that they continue to influence us today.

Rabbi Akiva is the inspiration and the role model for all Kabbalists since his time—the first and second centuries CE. Following Rabbi Akiva came Rabbi Shimon Bar-Yochai (Rashbi), who gave us *The Book of Zohar*. Then, fourteen centuries later came Rabbi Isaac Luria (The Holy Ari), whose legacy is *The Tree of Life*; and last came Rabbi Yehuda Ashlag (Baal HaSulam), whose *The Study of the Ten Sefirot* is the one book without which a contemporary Kabbalah student cannot achieve spirituality.

These great Kabbalists adapted their texts to their generations. Hence, the language varies to suit their contemporaries' levels of perception. But the message is always the same—Rabbi Akiva's motto, "Love thy friend as thyself." This message guides us back to Abraham's message that only through unity and bonding will we defeat egoism, achieve the Creator, and find a life of physical and spiritual bliss.

Let us now explore the personal stories of these pillars of spirituality.

RABBI AKIVA

Rabbi Akiva lived in the first and second centuries CE; he was the most prominent sage of his time. He was a leading pedagogue, the foremost Kabbalist of his time, and participated in the writing of the essential spiritual texts of his time—the *Mishnah* and the *Halacha*. At the same time, he was the spiritual leader of the Bar-Kokheva revolt, and was the man who revealed to the world the law of love.

Until the age of forty, Rabbi Akiva was an illiterate shepherd who led an ordinary life. He never dreamed that one day all of this would change dramatically.

THE TURNING POINT

Until that turning point, Rabbi Akiva worked as the shepherd for Kalba Savua. Around age forty, he began to feel
an uncontrollable urge to know the meaning of life and
to discover the rules that govern it. At that time, he was
romantically involved with Rachel, the daughter of Kalba
Savua, one of the wealthiest and most respected men in
Jerusalem at the time. The girl's father was not happy
with his daughter's infatuation with a "simpleton." But
as the best stories go, love prevailed, and the lovers married against her father's will.

According to the Talmud (a commentary on the
Mishnah), it was Rachel who encouraged Rabbi Akiva to
leave his home and go study Kabbalah from the greatest
Kabbalists of the time. Her heart told her that only in this
way would her husband find the answer to his questions.
She made him swear he would not return before he has
attained the laws of the Upper World. And thus, with his
wife's blessings, Rabbi Akiva's spiritual path began.

Rabbi Akiva studied under three Kabbalists: Rabbi
Elazar, Rabbi Yehoshua, and Nahum, Man of Gamzu.
He climbed the rungs of the spiritual ladder degree by
degree, and slowly surpassed his teachers, finally becoming the leading Kabbalist of his generation.

Once he had learned all he could from his mentors,
Rabbi Akiva established his own seminary. Word of his
wisdom spread quickly, and 24,000 students from all
over the country came to learn from him.

DISCOVERING THE LAW OF LOVE

Rabbi Akiva's unique teaching methods established brotherly love among his students. The physical reality obeys the same law of love, the Creator, which governs the spiritual realms. Therefore, when a person operates according to the law of love, he or she is in balance with Nature and feels as whole and eternal as Nature. But when we act out of self-love instead of brotherly love, we suffer and feel unhappy.

Happiness or unhappiness don't come to us from outside ourselves; they are a direct result of our similarity to Nature (the Creator). The Creator gives us nothing but good things because He is a force of love. But if we are opposite from Him, we cannot receive them. This is the cause of every pain and misfortune in the world.

Rabbi Akiva discovered that the law of Nature, the law of love, is constant and unchanging. He learned that when we change our attitude to others, we suddenly feel the whole of reality change, too. He recognized that egoistic relationships are the cause of every form of suffering in the world.

The ego, or as Kabbalists call it, "self-love," locks us within the limited reality we sense, and doesn't let us into the eternal, spiritual realm of life. The only way to experience the eternal is by changing our attitude toward others. Rabbi Akiva summarized his findings in his famous maxim, "Love thy friend as thyself; this is a great rule in the Torah (teaching)."

THE BAR-KOKHEVA REVOLT

In the year 132 CE, under the leadership of Shimon Bar-Kokheva, the Kingdom of Judea rebelled against the Romans. It seemed as if they would be successful when the Romans were forced to retreat. In desperation, the Romans called for assistance, and when the fresh troops arrived, the balance of power shifted. The Romans destroyed everything on their path and conquered the Kingdom of Judea. Tens of thousands of Jews were killed, and those who were taken captive were sold to slavery.

Crushing Bar-Kokheva's rebellion was the beginning of one of the most meaningful periods in the history of Kabbalah. The physical ruin of Judea was a manifestation of its people's spiritual decline, and the clearest symbol of this waning was the building of the pagan city of Aelia Capitolina on the ruins of Jerusalem.

Kabbalists who continued to teach despite the ruin were tortured to death, and Rabbi Akiva would become one of these victims. He continued to teach and share Kabbalah wisdom until he, too, was seized by the Romans. They sent him off to Caesarea Prison, where he was brutally executed by the Roman commissioner.

TWO BLOWS TO RABBI AKIVA'S WORK

In the past 5,000 years or so, humanity experienced several outbreaks of egoism. Each outbreak manifested in people wanting more than they did before, and each changed the course of history.

The first outbreak occurred in Babel, at the time of Abraham. The second was during Moses' time, and the third was during Rabbi Akiva's time. As a result of this last burst of egoism, the brotherly love among Rabbi Akiva's students was overthrown by unfounded hatred. This led to the spiritual decline of his students, who were no longer able to perceive the spiritual world, but were limited to perceiving only this world.

After the students fell into unfounded hatred, they suffered another blow. They were struck by a plague, killing all but five of Rabbi Akiva's 24,000 students. The remaining five survived because they had retained their sense of brotherly love. One of the five survivors of the plague was the man who was to continue Rabbi Akiva's teaching and put it to writing. His name was Rabbi Shimon Bar-Yochai, who would later write The Book of Zohar.

RABBI SHIMON BAR-YOCHAI (RASHBI)

Rabbi Shimon Bar-Yochai (Rashbi) received, through his mentor, Rabbi Akiva, 3,000 years of accumulated spiritual knowledge—all acquired by Kabbalists before him. After he wrote it down, he hid it, as humanity was not yet ready for it. Today, according to prominent Kabbalists such as Rabbi Yehuda Ashlag and The Vilna Gaon (GRA), we are indeed ready for the revelation of The Book of Zohar.

Rashbi, author of The Book of Zohar (The Book of Radiance) was a Tana—a great sage in the early Common

Era centuries. He was also Rabbi Akiva's direct disciple. Numerous legends have been told about Rashbi, who was mentioned repeatedly in the Talmud and in the Midrash, the sacred Hebrew texts of his time.

Rashbi was born and raised in the Galilee. He lived in Sidon (a city in today's Lebanon) and in Meron (in the north of Israel), and established a seminary in the Western Galilee, not far from Meron.

Even as a child, he was different from other children his age. Questions such as, "What is the purpose of my life?" "Who am I?" and "How is the world built?" haunted him, demanding that he discover the answers.

In those days, life in Galilee was harsh: the Romans who had killed his teacher, Rabbi Akiva, still persecuted Jews and continually invented new laws to punish them. Among these laws was one that prohibited Jews from studying Kabbalah.

But despite the Romans' prohibition, Rashbi immersed himself in Kabbalah studies and tried to understand its intricacies. He felt that beneath the Biblical stories lay a profound, hidden meaning that held the answers to his persistent questions.

Gradually, Rashbi came to realize that he had to find a teacher who had already traversed the spiritual path, gained experience, and could guide him up the spiritual ladder. This prompted him to join Rabbi Akiva's group, a decision that would be the turning point in Rashbi's life.

FROM STUDENT TO FUGITIVE

Rashbi was an avid, devoted student, burning with the desire to discover the Upper Force. He studied with Rabbi Akiva for thirteen years, and achieved the highest degree on the spiritual ladder.

The Bar-Kokheva revolt against the Roman rule in the land of Israel abruptly ended the great days of Rabbi Akiva's seminary. Rashbi joined the revolt and became one of its leaders, and after he learned how his teacher, Rabbi Akiva, had been executed, his resistance became even fiercer.

The Talmud says that once, when Rashbi spoke against the Roman rule, someone overheard him and notified the Roman authorities. The Romans tried Rashbi in his absence and sentenced him to death. But to execute Rashbi, they had to seize him first. The Roman emperor sent men to search for him, but to their disappointment, Rashbi seemed to have completely vanished.

THE CAVE AT PIQIIN

According to tradition, Rashbi and his son fled to Piqiin, a village in the north of Israel, where they hid in a cave and delved into the secrets of the wisdom of Kabbalah, where they discovered the entire system of creation.

After thirteen years in the cave, Rashbi heard that the Roman emperor had died. Finally, he could heave a sigh of relief. After leaving the cave, Rashbi gathered nine students and went with them to another small cave, known as The Idra Raba (The Great Assembly), not far from the village of Meron. With their help, he wrote *The Book of Zohar*, the most important book of Kabbalah.

הָאִדְרָא
שֶׁל
· רַבִּי שִׁמְעוֹן בַּר יוֹחַי ·
· וְר' יוֹסֵי·וְר' חִזְקִיָּהוּ בֶּן רָב ·
· וְר' יֵיסָא בֶּן יַעֲקֹב·וְר' יְהוּדָה ·
· וְר' אַבָּא·וְר' אֶלְעָזָר · וְר' יִצְחָק ·
· וְר' חִיָּיא · וְר' יֵיסָא ·

The sign at the entrance to Rashbi's secret cave, stating its name—The Assembly—and the names of the members of his group.

Kabbalist Rabbi Yehuda Ashlag described Rashbi and his students as the only people who achieved perfection—the 125 spiritual degrees that complete the correction of the soul. When he finished his commentary on *The Book of Zohar*, Ashlag held a festive meal to celebrate its completion. At that celebration, he stated that "...prior to the days of the Messiah, it was impossible to be awarded all 125 degrees... except for the Rashbi and his contemporaries, the authors of *The Book of Zohar*. They were awarded all 125 degrees in completeness, even though they lived prior to the days of the Messiah."

This is why it is often written in *The Book of Zohar* that there will not be a generation such as Rashbi's until "the generation of the Messiah King," (the time when all of humanity is corrected). This is why Rabbi Shimon's composition made such a mark in the world, since the spiritual secrets in it extend to all 125 degrees.

ONE IN MILLIONS

Rashbi was a unique soul, whose task was to help every creature connect with the **Upper Force**. This kind of soul comes down into our world and dresses as the greatest Kabbalists. Each time such a soul appears, it promotes humanity to a new spiritual degree and leaves its mark in Kabbalah books, which serve the following generations.

"This composition, called *The Book of Zohar*, is like Noah's Ark: there were many kinds, but those kinds and families could not exist unless by entering the ark. ... Thus the righteous will enter the secret of the Light of this composition to persist, and thus is the virtue of the composition, that immediately when engaging ...it will draw him as a magnet draws the iron. And he will enter it to save his soul and spirit and his correction."

--The Rav Kook, *Ohr Yakar (Bright Light)*

The Book of Zohar is undoubtedly one of the world's most renowned compositions. It has been the topic of thousands of stories, and although it was written almost two thousand years ago, the book is still shrouded in mystery. The fascination around it is so great that even though the book is completely incomprehensible to our generation without proper interpretation, millions of people diligently attempt to probe its secrets.

ISAAC LURIA (THE HOLY ARI)
1534-1572

Within a mere year and half, Isaac Luria (the Holy Ari) revolutionized Kabbalah and made it accessible to all. Since his time, his "Lurianic Kabbalah" has become the predominant approach to the study of Kabbalah.

The Ari was the greatest Kabbalist in 16th century Safed, a town near Rashbi's village, Meron. In the Ari's time, Safed was famed for its Kabbalist population.

The story of the Ari's life is shrouded in mystery and legends. One such legend is that when he was born, his father was told that his son was destined for greatness. The Ari's sudden demise at age thirty-eight, when he was in his prime, is still a mystery today.

A MAN OF MYSTERY AND LEGEND

The Ari was born in Jerusalem in 1534. At the age of eight, he lost his father, and his family was left destitute. Driven by despair, his mother decided to send young Isaac to live with his uncle in Egypt, where he spent most of his life.

As a young boy, the Ari would confine himself to his room for hours or even days at a time. He would immerse himself in *The Book of Zohar*, trying to understand its subtleties. Many folk stories claim that the Ari was awarded "the revelation of Elijah" (a unique spiritual revelation), and that he learned *The Zohar* "from him." To the Ari, *The Book of Zohar* was the whole world.

As the capital of Kabbalist studies in the 16th century, Safed attracted many practitioners from near and far. Additionally, Safed is located not far from Mt. Meron, the burial place of Rabbi Shimon Bar-Yochai, and in close vicinity to Rashbi's cave, the Idra Raba.

In the year 1570, a harsh winter struck Egypt. Torrential rains created massive flash floods, gale force winds tore rooftops off homes, and the Nile spilled over its banks, inundating whole villages under a deluge of mud and water.

One legend has it that Prophet Elijah visited the Ari on one of the stormiest nights of that dreadful winter and told him, "Your end is near. Leave here; take your family and go to the town of Safed, where you are eagerly awaited. There, in Safed, you will find your disciple, Chaim Vital. You will convey your wisdom to him, anoint him after you, and he will take your place."

Thus, in the dead of winter, the Ari went to Safed, in the land of Israel. He was thirty-six at the time, and he had two years left to live.

PREPARING FOR THE REVELATION

Kabbalists kept the wisdom of Kabbalah hidden for 1,500 years prior to the Ari, ever since Rashbi had concealed *The Book of Zohar*. They would rise at midnight, light a candle and shut the windows so their voices would not be heard outside. Then they would reverently open the Kabbalah books and delve into them, striving to grasp their hidden truths. Kabbalists were reluctant to publicize their work because they feared it would be misinterpreted. *The Book of Zohar* stated that it would reappear when the generation was ready, and at the time of the Ari, Kabbalists felt that the time was not yet ready.

Humanity had been waiting for many centuries for the right guide to open the gates of the wisdom of Kabbalah to the public. Finally, with the arrival of the Ari in Safed and the public's subsequent exposure to *The Book of Zohar*, it appeared that it was finally time to introduce the secrets of Kabbalah to the world.

Curiously, around the time of the Ari, and without any evident direct connection, many people, specifically artists and intellectuals, developed a keen interest in Kabbalah. One of these people was Giovanni Pico della Mirandola (1463-1494), an Italian scholar. His book, *Conclusions*, contains the following statement: "This true interpretation of the law ... which was revealed to Moses in godly tradition is called Kabbalah... which to Hebrews is the same as for us 'receiving.'"

It is difficult to overstate the Ari's importance and stature. Within merely eighteen months, he had left a huge mark on the history of Kabbalistic thought and teaching methods. His teachings introduced a new, systematic presentation of the spiritual knowledge. Using the Ari's method, anyone in today's scientific age can achieve what only a chosen few could achieve before.

Among the Ari's books, *The Tree of Life* is probably the most important. This book presents the Ari's teachings in a clear and simple style. Over the years, *The Tree of Life* has become one of the essential texts in Kabbalah, second only to *The Book of Zohar*.

The Ari passed away at age thirty-eight after falling ill with a plague that broke out in the summer of 1572. His appearance was a forerunner to a whole new era. He was not only one of the greatest Kabbalists, but also one of the first to be given "permission from Above" to disclose the wisdom of Kabbalah to the world. His ability to transform Kabbalah from a method for a chosen few to a method for all, made him a spiritual giant for the ages. Today, many more souls are ready for spiritual ascension, and to do so, they need to learn his method, the Lurianic Kabbalah.

RABBI YEHUDA LEIB HALEVI ASHLAG (BAAL HASULAM) 1884-1954

Rabbi Yehuda Ashlag is better known as Baal HaSulam (Owner of the Ladder) for his *Sulam* (Ladder) commentary on *The Book of Zohar*. Baal HaSulam spent his entire life interpreting the wisdom of Kabbalah, innovating and spreading it throughout Israel and the world at large. He adapted the Ari's Lurianic Kabbalah to our generation, and in doing so enabled everyone to study the roots of the reality in which we live, and thus perceive life's ultimate purpose.

Because Baal HaSulam was born when the world was ready to know about Kabbalah, his writings carry a distinct "multinational" nature. He predicted processes such as the fall of Russia's communism and globalization long before they became evident to the rest of us, and presented them in context with humanity's spiritual correction.

Baal HaSulam was born in Warsaw, Poland and studied Kabbalah with Rabbi Yehoshua of Porsov. In 1921, he immigrated with his family to Israel (which was then called Palestine) and settled in the Old City of Jerusalem.

The rumor of his arrival quickly spread throughout the city and he soon became known for his knowledge in Kabbalah. Gradually, a group of students formed around him, who would arrive at his home in the wee hours of the morning to study Kabbalah. Subsequently, Baal HaSulam moved from the Old City of Jerusalem to another Jerusalem neighborhood, Givat Shaul, where he served as the neighborhood rabbi for several years.

HIS MAJOR WORKS

His two principal works, the fruit of long years of labor, are *The Study of the Ten Sefirot*, based on the writings of the Ari, and *The Book of Zohar with the Sulam (Ladder) Commentary*. The publication of the sixteen parts of *The Study of the Ten Sefirot* began in 1937. *The Book of Zohar with the Sulam Commentary* was published in eighteen volumes between 1945-1953. Subsequently, Baal HaSulam wrote three additional volumes in which he interpreted

The New Zohar. The publication of the latter interpretation was completed in 1955, after his demise.

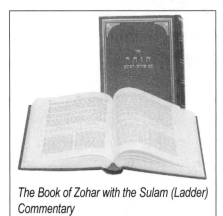

The Book of Zohar with the Sulam (Ladder) Commentary

In the introduction to his commentary on *The Book of Zohar,* he explained why he called it "The Ladder." "I have called my interpretation *The Sulam (Ladder),* to show that the role of my commentary is as the role of any ladder: if you have an attic filled with goodly matters, you need only a ladder to climb it, and all the abundance of the world is in your hands."

Baal HaSulam composed a series of introductions that initiate the student into effective study of Kabbalah texts, and clarify the study method. These include "The Preface to The Book of Zohar," "Introduction to The Book of Zohar," "Preface to the Wisdom of Kabbalah," "Preface to The Sulam Commentary," "A General Preface to The Tree of Life," and "Introduction to The Study of the Ten Sefirot."

In 1940, Baal HaSulam published a paper he called *The Nation.* In his last years, he wrote *The Writings of the Last Generation,* in which he analyzed different types of government, and outlined a detailed plan for building the corrected society for the future.

SPREADING THE WORD

Baal HaSulam did not settle for simply putting his ideas on paper. Instead, he worked arduously to promote them. As part of his efforts, he met with prominent figures in Israel such as David Ben Gurion, the first Prime Minister of Israel, Chaim Nachman Bialik, Zalman Shazar, and many others.

Ben Gurion wrote in his diaries that he met with Baal HaSulam several times, and that these meetings surprised him because "I wanted to talk to him about Kabbalah, and he, about socialism."

"Indeed we have already come to such a degree that the whole world is considered one collective and one society. Meaning, because each person in the world sucks his life's marrow and his livelihood from all the people in the world, he is forced to serve and care for the well-being of the whole world. ... The possibility of making good, happy, and peaceful conducts in one state is inconceivable when it is not so in all the countries in the world."

--Baal HaSulam, "Peace in the World"

An excerpt from the newspaper *Haaretz*, published December 16, 2004: "One day in Jerusalem of the early 1950s, Shlomo Shoham, later an Israel prize-winning author and criminologist, set out to look for Kabbalist Rabbi Yehuda Ashlag. ...Ashlag at that time was trying to print *Hasulam* (literally, *The Ladder*), his Hebrew translation and commentary on *The Book of Zohar*... Whenever he would raise a little money, from small donations, he would print parts of his *Hasulam*.

'I found him standing in a dilapidated building, almost a shack, which housed an old printing press. He couldn't afford to pay a typesetter and was doing the typesetting himself, letter by letter, standing over the printing press for hours at a time, despite the fact that he was in his late sixties. Ashlag was clearly a *Tzadik* (righteous man)—a humble man, with a radiant face. But he was an absolutely marginal figure and terribly impoverished. I later heard that he spent so many hours setting type that the lead used in the printing process damaged his health.'"

It took over half a century for his greatness to be recognized, but today his achievements are well known. In recent years, his teaching has attracted a great deal of attention, and hundreds of thousands of people throughout the world study his works, which have been translated into many different languages. Now, anyone who truly wishes to climb to the spiritual world can easily do so.

Baal HaSulam was a fascinating and complex individual, broadminded and well-educated. He was very much involved in global events as well as in the events that occurred in Israel, where he lived. His views are considered revolutionary and far-reaching in their boldness, even today

Baal HaSulam passed away in 1954, but his ideas have been perpetuated by his successor, his firstborn son, Rabbi Baruch Shalom Ashlag.

PART TWO

The (Gist of the) Wisdom of Kabbalah

As we wrote in the beginning of Part One, reality is an internal matter, a reflection of our inner experiences. These experiences "project" themselves onto our consciousness, as if on a movie screen, so we think that they are real. Part Two will focus on the origin of these pictures and their purpose in our lives.

3
THE ORIGIN OF CREATION

Now that we have established the importance of the study of Kabbalah, it's time to learn some of its basic ideas. Even though the scope of this book does not allow for a thorough study of the spiritual worlds, by the end of this chapter you will have a solid enough basis to continue, should you want to study Kabbalah in depth.

THE SPIRITUAL WORLDS

Creation is made entirely of a desire to receive pleasure. This desire evolved in four phases, the last of which is called "a creature." This template structure of evolution of desires is the basis for everything that exists.

Figure 1 (p. 49) describes the five phases of the making of the creature. If we treat this process as a story, it will help us remember that the drawings describe changes in our emotions, and not places or objects.

THE **THOUGHT OF CREATION**

Before anything is created, it has to be thought out, planned. In this case, we are talking about Creation and the thought that caused Creation to happen. We call it "The Thought of Creation."

In the first chapter, we said that Abraham, who discovered the wisdom of Kabbalah and was the first to disseminate it, discovered that the universe was "obeying" a force of love and giving. Because he realized this was the force that created all of life, he called it "the Creator." Hence, in Kabbalah, the term "Nature" is interchangeable with the term, "Creator." He also said that the Creator's will is to give us a very special kind of gift: becoming like Him. Since His is the most perfect, omnipotent, omniscient state that can exist, and since He is a force of love, He wants to give us the best: Himself.

Figure 1 describes the Thought of Creation as a desire to give pleasure (called "Light") to the creatures. This is also the root of Creation, where we, and all of life began.

Kabbalists use the term *Kli* (vessel, receptacle) to describe the desire to receive the pleasure, the Light. The vessel is the spiritual sense, the tool that perceives the Creator. Now we can see why Kabbalists called their wisdom "the wisdom of Kabbalah" (the wisdom of receiving).

There is also a good reason why Kabbalists called pleasure "Light." When the *Kli*—a creature, a person—feels the Creator, it is an experience of great wisdom that dawns on a person. When that happens to us, we realize that the newly manifested wisdom has always been there, but was hidden. It's as if the night's darkness has turned to daylight and the invisible has been made visible. Because this Light brings knowledge with it, Kabbalists called it "Light of Wisdom," and the method to receive it, "the wisdom of Kabbalah."

FOUR BASIC PHASES (AND THEIR ROOT)

Let's go back to our story of creation. To put the Thought of Creation into practice, the Creator designed a Creation that specifically wants to receive the pleasure of being identical to the Creator. If you're a parent, you know how that feels. What warmer words can someone say to a proud father than, "Your son's the spitting image of you!"?

As we've just said, the Thought of Creation—to give pleasure to the creature—is the root of Creation. For this reason, the Thought of

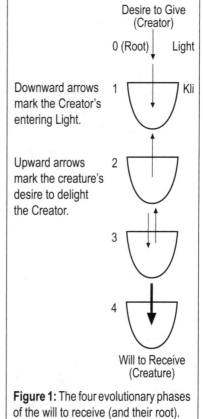

Figure 1: The four evolutionary phases of the will to receive (and their root).

Creation is called "the Root Phase" or "Phase Zero." The desire to receive the pleasure is called "Phase One."

Note that Phase Zero is shown as a downward arrow. Whenever an arrow points down, it means that Light comes from the Creator to Creation. But the opposite is not true: an upward arrow doesn't mean that Creation gives Light to the Creator, but that it *wants* to give back to Him. What happens when there are two arrows pointing in opposite directions? Keep reading and you'll soon find out.

Kabbalists refer to the Creator as "the Will to Bestow," and to the creature as "the will to receive delight and pleasure" or simply "the will to receive." We will talk about our perception of the Creator later, but what's important at this point is that Kabbalists always tell us what *they* perceive. They don't tell us that the Creator has a desire to give; they tell us that they see that the Creator has a desire to give, and that this is why they called Him "the Will to Bestow." Because they also discovered in themselves a desire to receive the pleasure He wants to give, they called themselves, "the will to receive."

So the will to receive is the first creation, the root of every single creature. When Creation, the will to receive, feels that the pleasure comes from a giver, she senses that real pleasure lies in giving, not in receiving. As a result, the will to receive begins to want to give (note the upward arrow extending from the second *Kli*—the cup in the drawing). This is a whole new phase—Phase Two.

Let's examine what distinguishes Phase Two from Phase One. If we examine Figure 1, we will see that the *Kli* itself doesn't change throughout the phases. This means that the will to receive is unchanging. Because the will to receive was designed in the Thought of Creation, it is eternal and can never be changed.

What does change, however, is *what* the *Kli* wants to receive. In Phase Two, the will to receive wants to receive pleasure from *giving*, not from receiving, and this is a fundamental change. The fundamental difference is that Phase Two needs another being to whom it can give. Therefore, to be a giver, Phase Two has to relate positively to someone or something else besides itself.

In Kabbalah, a giving degree is considered male and a receiving degree is considered female. Within each degree there are states in which it is acting as male or as female; hence, we sometimes refer to a certain degree as male, and sometimes as female, even within the same paragraph. The only two exceptions to this rule are the Creator, who is always male, being the source, and Creation, which is always female, since she receives from Him.

Phase Two, which forces us to give despite our underlying desire to receive, is what makes life possible. Without it, parents wouldn't care for their children and social life would have been impossible. For example, if I owned a restaurant, my underlying desire would be to make money. But to do so, I would be feeding strangers whom I have real no desire to benefit. The same is true for bankers, sales persons, and even cab drivers.

Now we can see why Nature's law is that of altruism and giving, not the law of receiving, even though the will to receive lies at the basis of every creature's motivation, as dictated by the Thought of Creation. From the minute we have both a desire to receive and a desire to give within Creation, everything that will happen to her will stem from reciprocity, the "relationship" between Phases One and Two.

Because the will to receive is opposite from the Creator's will to bestow, it is what distinguishes and separates us from the Creator. But the Creator didn't just create us opposite from Him; He also gave us a way to bridge the gap, and this is what we learn in the wisdom of Kabbalah.

As we've just shown, the new desire to give in Phase Two forces Creation to communicate, to seek someone who needs to receive. Therefore, Phase Two begins to examine what and how it can give to the Creator. After all, to whom else could it give?

But when Phase Two actually tries to give, it discovers that all the Creator wants is to give. He has absolutely no desire to receive. Besides, what can Creation give to the Creator?

Moreover, Phase Two discovers that at its core, its real desire is to receive. It discovers that its root is essentially a will to receive delight and pleasure, and there is not an ounce of genuine desire to bestow within it.

However, because the Creator only wants to give, Creation's will to receive is precisely what she *can* give to the Creator. By receiving, Creation discovers, she will actually be giving pleasure to the Creator, since giving is what pleases Him.

This may sound confusing, but if you think of the pleasure a mother derives from nurturing her baby, you will realize that the baby is actually giving pleasure to its mother simply by receiving the nurturing.

Hence, in Phase Three, Creation—the will to receive—*chooses* to receive. In so doing, she gives back to Root Phase, to the Creator.

Now we have a complete cycle where both players are givers. In Phase Zero, the Creator gives to Creation (Phase One). And in Phase Three, Creation, having gone through Phases One and Two, gives back to the Creator by receiving from Him.

In Figure 1, Phase Three is described as a *Kli* with two arrows, one pointing up and the other pointing down. The downward arrow indicates that Phase Three receives, as in Phase One, and the upward arrow indicates that its *intention* is to give, as in Phase Two.

Once again, both actions use the same will to receive as in Phases One and Two. This doesn't change at all. What does change is the intention with which Phase Three receives: in Phase One, it receives without thinking about it, but in Phase Three it receives in order to please the Creator.

As we've seen before, our egoistic intentions are the reason for all the problems in the world. Here, too, at the root of Creation, the intention is much more important than the action itself. To demonstrate this hierarchy, Baal HaSulam metaphorically says that Phase Three is ten percent receiving and ninety percent giving.

PHASE FOUR – CRAVING THE CREATOR'S MIND

Now it seems we have a perfect cycle where the Creator has succeeded in making the creature identical to Himself—a giver. Moreover, Creation enjoys this giving, and thus pleases the Creator.

But does this complete the Thought of Creation? Not quite. In a sense, we can say about Creation that she can walk His walk and talk His talk, but she cannot think His Thought. The act of reception (in Phase One) and the understanding that the Creator's only wish is to give (in Phase Two) make Creation *want* to be in the Creator's state, which is Phase Three.

But becoming a giver like the Creator doesn't mean that Creation has achieved the Creator's state. To complete the Thought of Creation, she must achieve the Creator's *thought*, not just His actions. In such a state, she would understand *why* the Creator formed her. Clearly, the desire to understand the Thought of Creation is an entirely new phase. The only thing we can compare it to is a child who wants to be both as strong and as wise as its parents. We instinctively know that this is possible only when the child matures and steps into his or her parents' shoes. This is why parents so often say to their kids, "Wait until you have children of your own; then you'll understand."

In Kabbalah, understanding the Thought of Creation—the deepest level of understanding—is called "attainment." This is what the will to receive craves in Phase Four.

One of the most common terms in Kabbalah is *Sefirot*. The word comes from the Hebrew word, *Sapir* (sapphire) and each *Sefira* (singular for *Sefirot*) has its own Light. Also, each of the four phases is named after one or more *Sefira*. Phase Zero is named *Keter*, Phase One, *Hochma*, Phase Two, *Bina*, Phase Three, *Zeir Anpin*, and Phase Four, *Malchut*.

Actually, there are ten *Sefirot* because *Zeir Anpin* is composed of six *Sefirot*: *Hesed, Gevura, Tifferet, Netzah, Hod,* and *Yesod*. Therefore, the complete set of *Sefirot* is *Keter, Hochma, Bina, Hesed, Gevura, Tifferet, Netzah, Hod, Yesod,* and *Malchut*.

The desire to acquire the Thought of Creation is the most powerful force in Creation. It stands behind the whole process of evolution. Whether we are aware of it or not, the ultimate knowledge we all seek is the understanding of why the Creator does what He does. It is the same drive that urged Kabbalists to discover the secrets of Creation thousands of years ago. Until we understand it, we will have no peace of mind.

THE QUEST FOR THE
THOUGHT OF CREATION

Even though the Creator wants us to receive the pleasure of becoming identical to Him, He didn't give us this desire to begin with. All that He gave us—Creation—was an infinite craving for pleasure. However, as we can see in the sequence of phases, the Creator did not infuse Creation with a specific desire to be like Him. This evolved within her through the phases.

In Phase Three, Creation had already received everything and intended to give back to the Creator. The sequence could have ended right then and there, since she was already doing exactly what the Creator was doing—giving. In that sense, Creator and Creation were already identical.

But Creation did not settle for giving. She wanted to understand what made giving pleasurable, why a giving force was necessary to create reality, and what wisdom the giver obtained by giving. In short, Creation wanted to understand the Thought of Creation. This was a new craving that the Creator had not "planted" in her.

When Creation developed the desire to become like the Creator, she became a distinct, separated being from Him. We can look at it this way: If I want to be like someone else, it necessarily means that I'm aware that that someone else exists, and that that someone has something that I want. It may be that person's possession or a quality; but it is something that the other has, and which I would very much like to have, too.

In such a state, I not only realize that there is someone else besides me, but I realize that that someone is not only *different* from me, but *better, superior.* Otherwise, why would I want to be like Him?

Therefore, *Malchut*, Phase Four, is very different from the first three phases because it wants to receive a very specific kind of pleasure (hence the thicker arrow)—that of being identical to the Creator. From the Creator's perspective, *Malchut's* desire completes the Thought of Creation, the cycle that He originally had in mind (Figure 2).

As Figure 2 indicates, achieving the Thought of Creation will elevate *Malchut* (Creation) to a higher degree than its own

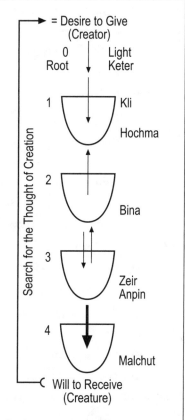

Figure 2: The arrow from *Malchut* to the Creator indicates *Malchut's* focused desire on becoming Creator-like by achieving His Thought.

root, a higher place than the Source that created it. Put simply, it would raise *Malchut* to the level of the Creator and make it identical to Him.

But alas, we are not looking at things from the Creator's perspective. From down here, with our broken spiritual spectacles, the picture is less than ideal. In order for Creation, who is completely opposite from the Creator, to become like the Creator, she must use her will to receive with the *intention* to bestow. By doing that, she will turn her focus from her own pleasure to the joy the Creator receives from giving. And in so doing, she, too, will become a giver.

Actually, in Phase Three, Creation already received in order to give to the Creator. So from the Creator's perspective, Phase Three had already completed the job of becoming identical to the Creator. The Creator gives in order to bestow, and Phase Three receives in order to bestow, so in that sense they are the same.

But the ultimate pleasure is not in knowing what the Creator does and replicating His actions. The ultimate pleasure is in knowing *why* He does what He does, acquiring the same *thoughts* as His, and even the same nature. And this knowledge—the Creator's nature—hasn't been given to Creation. It is what Creation (Phase Four) must achieve on her own.

There is a beautiful connection here. On the one hand, it seems as if we (Creation) and the Creator are on opposite sides of the court, because we receive what He gives. But in fact, His greatest pleasure is to see us becoming like Him, and our greatest pleasure would be to become like Him. Similarly, every child wants to become like its parents, and every parent naturally wants his or her child to achieve what the parent did not.

Therefore, we and the Creator are actually pursuing the same goal! If we could comprehend this concept, our lives would be very, very different. Instead of the confusion and disorientation so many of us experience today, we and the Creator could march together toward our designated goal since the dawn of Creation.

Kabbalists use many terms to describe "the will to bestow": Creator, Light, Giver, Thought of Creation, Phase Zero, Root, Root Phase, *Keter*, *Bina*, and many others.

Similarly, they use many terms to describe "the will to receive": Creation, creature, *Kli*, receivers, Phase One, *Hochma*, and *Malchut* are just a few.

These terms refer to subtleties in the two characteristics— bestowal and reception. If we remember that, we will not be confused by all the names.

To become like the Creator, a giver, the *Kli* does two things. First, it stops receiving altogether, an act called *Tzimtzum* (restriction). It stops the Light entirely and doesn't allow any of it into the *Kli*. Similarly, it's easier to avoid eating something tasty, but unhealthy, than to eat just a little and leave the rest on the plate. Therefore, making a *Tzimtzum* is the first and easiest step to becoming like the Creator. The ability to make the *Tzimtzum* is called "acquiring a *Masach* (screen)." Figure 3 shows how the Creator's Light approaches the *Kli* but is rejected by the *Masach*.

The next thing that *Malchut* does is to set up a mechanism that examines the Light (pleasure) and decides if it will receive it, and if so, how much. This mechanism is a development of the *Masach* (screen).

The condition by which the *Masach* determines how much to receive is called "aim to bestow." In simple terms, the *Kli* only takes in what it can receive with the intention to please the Creator, or as Kabbalists put it, "in order to bestow" (Figure 4). The Light received within the *Kli* is called "Inner Light," and the Light that remains outside is called "Surrounding Light."

At the end of the correction process, the *Kli* will receive all of the Creator's Light and unite with Him. This is the purpose of Creation. When we reach that state, we will feel it both as individuals and as a single, united society. This is because the complete *Kli* is not made of one person's desires, but of the desires of all of humanity. And when we complete this last correction, we will become identical to the Creator, Phase Four will be fulfilled, and Creation will be completed from our perspective, just as it is completed from His.

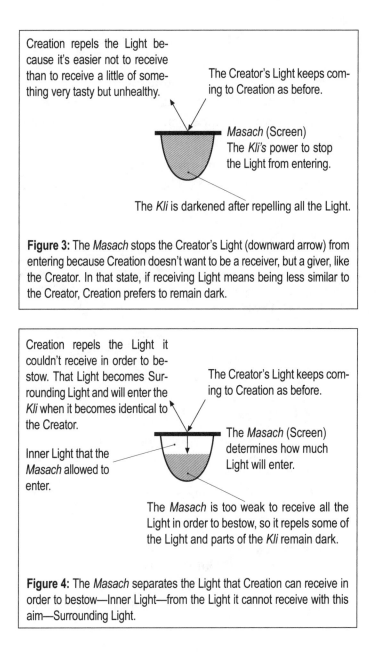

Creation repels the Light because it's easier not to receive than to receive a little of something very tasty but unhealthy.

The Creator's Light keeps coming to Creation as before.

Masach (Screen)
The *Kli's* power to stop the Light from entering.

The *Kli* is darkened after repelling all the Light.

Figure 3: The *Masach* stops the Creator's Light (downward arrow) from entering because Creation doesn't want to be a receiver, but a giver, like the Creator. In that state, if receiving Light means being less similar to the Creator, Creation prefers to remain dark.

Creation repels the Light it couldn't receive in order to bestow. That Light becomes Surrounding Light and will enter the *Kli* when it becomes identical to the Creator.

The Creator's Light keeps coming to Creation as before.

Inner Light that the *Masach* allowed to enter.

The *Masach* (Screen) determines how much Light will enter.

The *Masach* is too weak to receive all the Light in order to bestow, so it repels some of the Light and parts of the *Kli* remain dark.

Figure 4: The *Masach* separates the Light that Creation can receive in order to bestow—Inner Light—from the Light it cannot receive with this aim—Surrounding Light.

THE ROUTE

To carry out the task of becoming identical to the Creator, the first thing Creation must obtain is the right environment to evolve and become Creator-like. This environment is called "worlds."

At Phase Four, Creation was divided into two parts: upper and lower (Figure 5). The upper part constitutes the Upper (Spiritual) Worlds, and the lower part constitutes Creation, which is made of desires where the *Masach* did not allow the Light to enter.

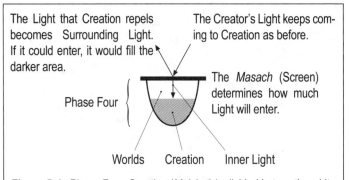

The Light that Creation repels becomes Surrounding Light. If it could enter, it would fill the darker area.

The Creator's Light keeps coming to Creation as before.

Phase Four

The *Masach* (Screen) determines how much Light will enter.

Worlds   Creation   Inner Light

Figure 5: In Phase Four, Creation (*Malchut*) is divided in two: the white zone indicates desires that can work in order to bestow, and hence receive Light. These constitute the Upper Worlds. The darker zone indicates desires that cannot work in order to bestow, and hence cannot receive Light. These constitute Creation.

USING THE SCREEN

Let's talk some more about Phase Four and how it works with the *Masach*. After all, Phase Four is our root, so if we understand how it works, we might learn something about ourselves.

Upper and Lower

We already know that Creation is made of one thing only: a will to receive delight and pleasure. Therefore, upper and lower do not relate to places, but to desires that we relate to as higher or lower. In other words, higher desires are desires we appreciate more than the desires we consider inferior. In the case of Phase Four, any desire that can be used to bestow upon the Creator belongs in the upper part, and any desire that can't be used in this way belongs in the lower part.

Phase Four, *Malchut*, evolved from Phase Three, which evolved from Phase Two, etc.. Similarly, Abraham Lincoln wasn't born president of the United States of America. He grew from baby Abe to a child, then to a youth, and finally to an adult who one day became Mr. President.

But Abe's early stages did not disappear when he became president. Without them, President Lincoln would not have become President Lincoln. The reason we can't see them is because the most developed level dominates and overshadows the less developed. But the last, highest level, not only feels the other levels within it, it works with these other levels. This is why we sometimes feel like children, especially when touched in places in our personalities where we haven't matured. These places are not covered by a grownup layer, and those soft spots make us feel as defenseless as children.

Nevertheless, this multi-layered structure is what enables us to eventually become parents. In the process of raising children, we combine our past and present phases. We understand the situations our children experience because we've had similar experiences, and we can relate to those situations with the knowledge and experience we've accumulated through life.

The reason we are built this way is that *Malchut* (Creation, Phase Four, us) is built in exactly the same way. All of *Malchut's* previous phases exist within it and help sustain its structure.

To become as similar to the Creator as possible, *Malchut* analyzes each level of desire within itself and splits these desires into workable and unworkable ones within each level. The workable desires will be used to receive in order to give to the Creator, as well as "help" the Creator complete His task of making *Malchut* identical to Him.

A few pages back, we said that to carry out the task of becoming identical to the Creator, the creature must create the right environment to evolve and become Creator-like. That's exactly what the worlds—workable desires—do. They "show" the unworkable desires how to receive in order to bestow upon the Creator, and in so doing, help the unworkable desires correct themselves.

We can picture the relationship between the worlds and Creation as a group of construction workers, where one of the workers doesn't know what to do. The worlds teach Creation by demonstrating how to do each task: how to drill, how to use a hammer, a level, and so on.

In the case of spirituality, the worlds show Creation what the Creator has given them and how they work with it in the right way. Bit by bit, Creation can begin to use her desires in this way, too.

From all we've learned so far, we still don't know which of the five worlds we talked about is our physical world. Actually, none of them is ours. Keep in mind that there are no "places" in spirituality, only states. The higher the world, the more altruistic a state it represents. The reason our world isn't mentioned anywhere is that the spiritual worlds are altruistic, and our world is, like us, egoistic. Because egoism is opposite to altruism, our world is detached from the system of the spiritual worlds. This is why Kabbalists did not mention it in the structure they depicted in their books.

WORKABLE AND UNWORKABLE DESIRES

Earlier in this chapter we said that the four-phase pattern is the basis for everything that exists. Therefore, when the desires were split into those that could receive Light, and those that couldn't, they followed the same four-phase pattern. The desires that could receive Light are called "workable desires," and desires that can't receive Light are called "unworkable desires."

The workable desires created the Upper Worlds, and the unworkable desires created Creation, and later our world (Figure 6). The workable desires at the Root Phase created the world *Adam Kadmon*, and the unworkable ones, which remained dark (without Light) were called "still," and formed the still (unchanging) level of Creation.

Workable desires at Phase One created the world *Atzilut*, and the unworkable ones remained dark and constitute the "Vegetative" level of Creation. Workable desires at Phase Two created the world *Beria*, and the unworkable ones constitute the "Animate" level of Creation. Similarly, workable desires at Phase Three constitute the world *Yetzira*, and the unworkable ones constitute the "Speaking" level of Creation. And finally, workable desires at Phase Four constitute the world *Assiya*, and unworkable ones remained dark and constitute the "Spiritual" level of Creation.

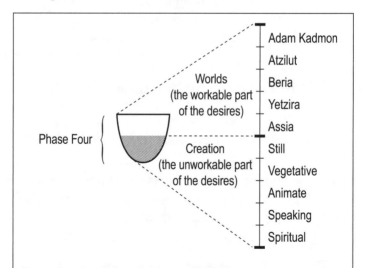

Figure 6: In Phase Four, desires are divided into workable desires and unworkable desires. The workable desires create the Upper Worlds, and the unworkable desires create Creation. The Upper Worlds' task is to "teach" Creation how to receive in order to bestow.

Note that the strongest desires, the most egoistic and seemingly most remote from the Creator, are called "spiritual." Just as in the four phases, the most powerful desire wishes to become like the Creator. Hence, only the last degree, which is seemingly the darkest and most egoistic, can develop a desire to be like the Creator and achieve spirituality.

It turns out that Creation is the only part that still needs to be "worked on," so it can receive Light. Let us learn how Creation evolved, how it became our world, and how we can correct it.

It is important to remember that the Upper Worlds do not actually exist until we discover them as we develop our spiritual perception as we become like the Creator. The reason Kabbalists speak of these worlds in past tense is that they wrote their books for us *after* they climbed from our world to the spiritual worlds, and then told us what they had found. To reveal the Upper Worlds, we, too, must climb there and see for ourselves. The only way to do that is by becoming similar to the Creator—altruistic.

THE COMMON SOUL

The actual root of everything that happens here in our world is called "the common soul," or as Kabbalists refer to it, *Adam ha Rishon* (The First Man). *Adam ha Rishon* is a structure of desires that emerged once the formation of the spiritual worlds was completed.

Once the five worlds, *Adam Kadmon, Atzilut, Beria, Yetzira,* and *Assiya* completed their development of the upper part of Phase Four, it was time to develop the lower part. *Adam ha Rishon,* which we know as "Adam," is made of unworkable desires that couldn't receive Light in order to give to the Creator when they were first created. If you look back at Figure 6, Adam is the next step in the development of Creation, and consists of the parts shown in the grey area in the drawing. The unworkable desires in that part, which formed the still, vegetative, animate, speaking, and spiritual, must now surface one by one and become corrected, or workable.

To do that, these desires will need the help of the worlds, the workable desires. This is why *Adam ha Rishon* evolves by the same degrees as did the worlds and the four basic phases.

THE GREAT FALL

But with Adam, matters aren't as straightforward as they were with the Upper Worlds. Although Adam is unaware of it, his desires are egoistic, self-centered; this is why he couldn't receive Light to begin with. When he followed the example of the Upper Worlds and tried to receive Light, the pleasure of the Light was overwhelming and he wanted to receive it for himself.

Recall that when Phase Four realized she wanted to become like the Creator, the first thing she did was to abstain from receiving Light for her own pleasure, in an act called *Tzimtzum* (restriction). Adam's present attempt to receive the Light despite the *Tzimtzum* was an attempt to revoke that decision. As a result, the *Tzimtzum* was reinforced in full power, and the *Masach* (screen) immediately repelled all the Light that Adam had received.

The repelling of the Light in Adam's case is very different from the original *Tzimtzum*. When the *Tzimtzum* first occurred, it was a step forward from a state of reception without any consideration of the giver, the Creator. In Adam's case, however, the pleasure made him "blot out" the Creator from his consciousness so he could receive the Light for himself without having to think of the Creator's joy. This made Adam *less* like the Creator—the force of love and giving—than prior to his receiving the Light. This is why Adam's attempt to receive Light for himself is considered a sin: it drives him away from the purpose of creation.

The Kabbalistic term for a "sin" is "breaking." Thus, *Adam ha Rishon* broke. Kabbalists explain that Adam's soul broke into 600,000 pieces. Each piece was a result of Adam's egoistic attempt, and hence was egoistic, too. An egoistic element is detached from the Creator because it is opposite from Him. This is how our world was created, where the egoistic desires rule and the Creator is hidden from sight by our own egoism.

Adam wasn't born an egoist; he only discovered his egoism when he tried to use his desires to receive the Light. His intention was to receive in order to bestow, just like the worlds had shown him. But his failure taught him that he was different from them, that he was essentially egoistic and had to be corrected before he could receive, as did the worlds.

The shattering of Adam's soul into many pieces was actually a good thing. In breaking, the great egoistic desire was split into many little pieces of smaller desires, which are easier to correct. Each such desire exists within each of us. When everyone in the world corrects their own share of Adam's soul, the whole of humanity will be corrected, one soul, receiving in order to bestow, at one with the Creator, and enjoying all the Light that He intended to give us in the Thought of Creation.

4
MENDING ADAM
TO ACHIEVE PERFECTION

In the beginning of Chapter Three, we wrote that before anything was created, there was the Thought of Creation. This Thought created Phases One through Four of the will to receive, which created the worlds *Adam Kadmon* through *Assiya*, which then created the soul of *Adam ha Rishon*, which broke into the myriad souls we have today.

It's very important to remember this order of creation because it reminds us that things evolve from above downward, from spiritual to corporeal, and not the other way around. In practical terms, it means that our world is created and governed by the spiritual worlds.

Moreover, there is not a single event in our world that doesn't happen above first. And the only difference between our world and the spiritual worlds is that events in the spiritual worlds reflect altruistic intentions, and events in our world reflect egoistic intentions.

Because of this cascading structure of the worlds, our world is called the "world of consequences" of spiritual processes and occurrences. Whatever we do here has no impact of any kind on the spiritual worlds. Therefore, if we want to change anything in our world, we must first climb to the spiritual worlds, the "control room" of our world, and affect our world from there.

Just as it happens in the spiritual worlds, everything in our world evolves along the same five stages from Zero to Four. Figure 7 focuses on the part of *Malchut's* desires that could not receive in order to bestow, and hence remained dark. The smallest desires create the still level of Creation, and the stronger the desires become, so does their activity level: from vegetative to animate to speaking, and finally, to human (spiritual).

However, it is important to remember that the desires in Figure 7 are inactive. They are *not* receiving Light, so they are doing no harm. They become active only when Adam tries to use them to receive Light. This is when their egoistic nature surfaces, and this is when they break. Hence, as long as they are inactive, they are still considered spiritual desires, because there is no active egoism to separate them from the Creator's quality of giving. They become detached from Him only when they are activated.

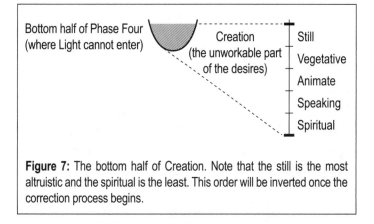

Figure 7: The bottom half of Creation. Note that the still is the most altruistic and the spiritual is the least. This order will be inverted once the correction process begins.

The still, vegetative, animate, speaking, and spiritual levels in our world are actually manifestations of desires that originate in the Upper World. They become physical only when they are activated in the wrong way—egoistically. If we could activate them in the right way, in order to please the Creator, we could use them to receive Light. This is the essence of the correction that we need to make here in this world.

Also, recall that we said that the still level is made of the smallest desires, the vegetative consists of stronger ones and so on through the strongest desire—the spiritual level. So when the desires break and begin to work selfishly, the weaker desires are the least broken, and the strongest desires suffer the worst shattering. Accordingly, the still (inanimate, mineral) level in our world is the least broken (egoistic); plants are more egoistic, animals are more egoistic than plants, and humans are the most egoistic of all.

THE PYRAMID

Because spiritual desires are divided into stronger and weaker, our world is built like a pyramid. The weakest desires are the least egoistic and form the base level of Creation, the still (Figure 8). Above these, and relying on them, is the vegetative level. In a sense, the vegetative is exploiting the still because they are nourished by minerals and water, which belong to the still level of our world.

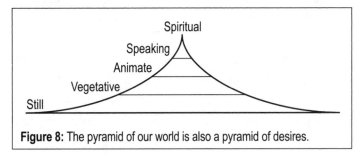

Figure 8: The pyramid of our world is also a pyramid of desires.

Next in line is the animate level, which nurtures mostly on plants, "exploiting" them for their sustenance. Highest on the scale is the speaking (human) level, which feeds on both plants and animals, and some minerals.

The spiritual level isn't a separate level in its physical manifestation. Rather, it is a distinct level of development, a state where one's *soul* yearns to return to its root in the Upper Worlds, where it was in direct contact with the Creator. And here lies the uniqueness of the spiritual level: while it is the greatest, most egoistic desire, it is also the only level that really wants to bond with the Creator, the altruistic force of life. This is why the spiritual level in us is the one that makes us feel the lowest, but is also the key to our transformation from egoism to altruism.

THE MAKING OF LIFE

In his "Preface to the Wisdom of Kabbalah," one of his introductions to the *Sulam* commentary on *The Book of Zohar*, Baal HaSulam explains the difference between spirituality and corporeality. He says that anything that has an aim to bestow, like the Creator, is spiritual, and anything that has an aim to receive, opposite from the Creator, is corporeal. Prior to Adam's breaking, there was no such thing as an active aim to receive. Hence, his breaking also marks the first appearance of physical reality.

In Chapter Three, we said that the four-phase pattern continues through the whole of Creation. Our world is no exception to the rule. Hence, the first substance to appear was the still, or inanimate substance, representing the smallest level of desires.

Following the still, came vegetation, then animals, representing the animate level of desires, and finally humans—the physical manifestation of the speaking level. The last desire to appear was the desire for spirituality, for the Creator. As we've explained in the previous section, this last desire is both the most powerful, and the only one that can achieve the Creator (altruism).

Of course, things didn't go quite as quickly as we just described. First appeared the minerals, billions of trillions of tons of minerals, which gradually formed the galaxies, stars, and planets. Then, lost in these trillions of tons of matter, there appeared a tiny speck called "Planet Earth." And on this Earth appeared the vegetative level. Naturally, the vegetation on Earth is infinitely smaller in mass than that of the still matter on Earth, all the more so compared to the quantity of inanimate matter in the whole universe. The animate, which appeared after the vegetative, has a tiny mass, even compared to the vegetative. The speaking, of course, the last to appear, has the least mass of all.

The spiritual level appeared just "recently." Since we are speaking of geological times here, when we say recently, we mean that it emerged only a few thousand years ago.

The full size of Creation is incomprehensible. If we look at the pyramid of Creation (Figure 8) and think of the proportions between every two adjacent levels, we will begin to understand just how recent the desire for spirituality really is. If we "compress" the time the universe has existed—approximately fifteen billion years—into a single day of twenty-four hours, proportionally, the desire for spirituality appeared 0.0288 seconds ago. In geological terms, this is now.

Thus, on the one hand, the higher the desire, the rarer (and younger) it is. On the other hand, the existence of a spiritual level above the human level indicates that we haven't completed our evolution. Evolution is as dynamic as ever, but because we are the last level to appear, we naturally think we are the top level. We may be at the top level, but we are not at the final level. We are only at the last of the levels that have already emerged.

The final level will use our bodies as hosts, but will consist of entirely new ways of thinking, feeling and being. In this level, we will perceive reality very differently than we do today. It is already evolving within us, and it is called "the spiritual level."

No physical changes or new species will be required, just a transformation in our perception of the world. This is why the next phase in evolution is so elusive; it is within us. This phase will evolve whether or not we are aware of it. However, with awareness and active participation, we can rush its emergence and make it much more fascinating and enjoyable. The wisdom of Kabbalah teaches how we can become aware of the spiritual level within us, and participate in its evolvement in the most effective and beneficial way for us. It was for this purpose that Kabbalah was created.

AS ABOVE, SO BELOW

If we draw a parallel between the earthly phases and the four basic phases of Light, the still era corresponds to the Root Phase, the vegetative era corresponds to Phase One, the animate era to Phase Two, the speaking era to Phase Three, and the spiritual era to Phase Four.

Planet Earth's scorching youth lasted several billion years. As it cooled, vegetative life appeared and reigned over the planet for many more millions of years. But just as the mass of vegetation is much less than that of the still, the vegetative period was much shorter than Earth's inanimate period.

Following the completion of the vegetative phase, the animate period arrived. As with the previous two degrees, the animate era was much shorter than the vegetative era, matching the proportion between the vegetative and animate masses.

The human phase, which corresponds to the speaking level of the pyramid, has only been around for the past forty thousand years or so. When humanity completes its evolution of the fourth (and last) phase, evolution will be complete and humanity will reunite with the Creator.

The Fourth Phase began some five thousand years ago, when the desires for spirituality first appeared. In Kabbalah, the appearance of the desire for spirituality is called "the appearance of the point in the heart."

If if you examine the pyramid in Figure 8, you will find that we actually have a very broad-based pyramid here. Each level contains much more substance and lasts much longer than the one above it.

Nevertheless, each degree is totally subjugated and controlled by its adjacent superior. This is why the correction of the entire world depends on the correction of the last, and highest degree—the spiritual.

As in the spiritual world, the name of the person who first experienced the point in the heart was Adam. He was *Adam ha Rishon* (The First Man). The name, Adam, comes from the Hebrew words, *Adameh la Elyon—*

"I will be like the Most High" (Isaiah 14:14)—and reflects Adam's desire to be like the Creator.

The Point in the Heart

When Kabbalists write about the heart, they are not referring to the pump in our chests. The heart is the sum of our desires to receive pleasure, and the desire for spirituality is the "point in the heart." This point is very important because once it appears it sheds a new light on everything we experience and gives our lives a higher, spiritual meaning. This point in the heart is what eventually leads us to spirituality.

These days, at the start of the 21st century, evolution is completing its development of the Fourth Phase—the desire to be like the Creator. This is why today more and more people are looking for spiritual answers to their questions.

UP THE LADDER

When Kabbalists talk about spiritually evolving, they are referring to climbing up the spiritual ladder. This is why Kabbalist Yehuda Ashlag named his commentary on *The Book of Zohar, Perush HaSulam* (The Ladder Commentary), for which he was named Baal HaSulam (Owner of the Ladder). But climbing "up the ladder" actually means going "back to the roots." This is because the roots of our creation, the Upper Worlds, are a part of us. In a sense, we've already been there, even though we're unaware of it. Now we must figure out how to get back there by ourselves, consciously.

The root is our final goal, where we are ultimately heading. But to get there quickly and peacefully we need a great desire for it—a *Kli*. The desire for spirituality is what characterizes the spiritual level in our evolution.

Just as not all gifted athletes win medals, only those who are both gifted *and* highly motivated, to achieve spirituality, we need to be very highly motivated. To understand where highly motivated athletes get their motivation, we must look not only at the athletes, but at their environment. In many countries, there are special schools for athletes, where their lives revolve entirely around their sport, and their competitiveness is nurtured.

Similarly, to achieve spirituality, we must create an environment that will encourage us to be more spiritual. Such an environment will make us think that spirituality is the most important thing in life, and that by achieving it, we will be the happiest and most complete people on earth. Our friends will describe how great it is to be spiritual, united with the Creator, just as athletes' friends talk to them about winning this or that race, and what it feels like to be the first at the finish line etc.. In Kabbalah, we would say that "the medal shines" for athletes with "Surrounding Light."

Therefore, to want spirituality, we need to acquire the kind of Surrounding Light that will make us want spiritual pleasures. The more of this Light we gather, the faster we will progress. Wanting spirituality is called "raising MAN," and we can use the same technique that athletes use to increase the desire for a medal—picture it, talk about it, read about it, think about it, and do whatever we can to focus on it. But the most powerful means to increase any desire is still our social environment.

Is there a difference between "Surrounding Light" and just "Light"?

The different titles, "Surrounding Light" and "Light," relate to two functions of the same Light. Light that is *not* considered Surrounding is what we experience as pleasure, while Surrounding Light is the Light that builds our *Kli*, the place where the Light will finally enter. Both are actually one Light, but when we experience it as correcting and building, we call it "Surrounding Light." When we feel it as pure pleasure, we call it "Light."

In his "Introduction to the Study of the Ten Sefirot," Baal Ha-Sulam explains that until we develop a *Kli*, we do not receive any Light. But the Light is there, surrounding our souls, and gradually builds our *Kli* by increasing our desire for it.

We will talk about the environment more in Part Four, but for now, let's think of it in the following way: If everyone around me wants and talks about the same thing, and there's only one thing that's "in," I'm bound to want it. The more I want something, the greater are my efforts to obtain it, the more my *Kli* grows, and the greater the Surrounding Light that I will draw.

The growing *Kli* encourages me to develop new means to get what I want, thus progressing faster toward my goal. The equation is simple and straightforward: The bigger the *Kli*, the greater the Light; the greater the Light, the quicker the correction and the reception of the Light inside the *Kli*.

BUILDING THE VESSEL

We still need to understand how the Surrounding Light builds our *Kli* and why it is called "Light" to begin with. But to understand that, we must first understand the concept of *Reshimot*.

Recall that the spiritual worlds and the soul of *Adam ha Rishon* evolved in a certain order. In the worlds, it was *Adam Kadmon, Atzilut, Beria, Yetzira,* and *Assiya*. In *Adam ha Rishon*, the evolution was named after the kind of desire that emerged—still, vegetative, animate, speaking, and spiritual.

Just as we don't forget our childhood, but rely on the past during our present experiences, each completed step in the evolutionary process is not lost, but is registered in our unconscious "spiritual memory." In other words, within us lies the entire history of our spiritual evolution, from the time we were one with the Thought of Creation to this day. Going up the spiritual ladder simply means remembering the states we've already experienced.

These memories are aptly named *Reshimot* (records), and each *Reshimo* stands for a specific spiritual state. Because our spiritual evolution unfolded in a specific order, the *Reshimot* surface within us in just that order. In other words, our future states are already determined, and we are not creating anything new, just remembering and re-experiencing events that already happened to us. The one thing we can determine, which we will discuss at length in the following chapters, is how fast we can climb the ladder. The harder we work at climbing it, the faster these states will change and the faster we will spiritually progress.

Each *Reshimo* is completed when we have fully experienced it, and like a chain, when one *Reshimo* ends, the next *Reshimo* emerges. The *Reshimo* we are experiencing now (our present reality) is actually an offspring of the *Reshimo* that will appear next (my adjacent future state). But since now we're going back up the ladder, the present *Reshimo* awakens its original creator, its parent, if you will. Thus, we should never expect to end our present state and rest, because when one state ends it necessarily leads to the next in line until we complete our correction. Then we will rest in a state of eternal bliss.

Our efforts to become altruistic (spiritual) bring us closer to our corrected state because the greater Light that we draw awakens the *Reshimot* more quickly. And since those *Reshimot* are records of higher spiritual experiences, the sensations they create in us are more spiritual, too.

When that happens, we begin to vaguely sense the connectedness, unity, and love that exist in that state, much like a distant, faint light. The more we try to reach it, the closer we come to it and the brighter it shines. Moreover, the stronger the Light, the stronger is our desire for it. Thus, the Light builds our *Kli*, our desire for spirituality.

Now we also see that the name, "Surrounding Light," perfectly describes how we sense it. As long as we haven't reached it, we see it as external, attracting us with its blinding promise of bliss.

Every time the Light builds a big enough *Kli* for us to step to the next level, the next *Reshimo* comes along and a new desire emerges in us. We don't know why our desires change because they're always parts of *Reshimot* from a higher degree than our current level, even when they don't seem to be.

Just as our present *Reshimo* surfaced and brought us to our present state, the new desire that approaches comes from a new *Reshimo*, which will produce a new state. At the moment, we call that new *Reshimo* "our future." However, in a little while, when that *Reshimo* has emerged in its fullest, it will be our present, just as our current *Reshimo* is our present. This is how we continue our climb up the ladder. It is a spiral of *Reshimot* and ascents that end at the purpose of Creation—the root of our souls, when we are equal and united with the Creator.

THE DESIRE
FOR SPIRITUALITY

Before we focus on the desire for spirituality, let's see what Kabbalah has to say about our individual desires: The only difference between people is in the way they want to experience pleasure. Pleasure in itself, however, is amorphous, intangible. When we cover it with different "dresses," or "coatings," it creates an illusion that there are different kinds of pleasure, when in fact there are simply many kinds of coatings.

The fact that pleasure is essentially spiritual explains why we have an unconscious craving to replace the superficial coatings of the pleasure with the desire to feel it in its pure form: the Creator's Light.

And because we're unaware that the difference between people is in the coatings of pleasure they wish for, we judge them according to the coatings they prefer. We consider certain coatings of pleasure legitimate, such as love of children, while others, such as drugs, are considered unacceptable. When we feel an unacceptable coating for pleasure emerging in us, we are forced to conceal our desire for that coating. However, concealing a desire doesn't make it go away, and certainly doesn't correct it.

As we've explained above, the lower part of Phase Four is the substance of the soul of *Adam ha Rishon* (see Figure 6 on p. 66). Just as the worlds are built according to the growing desires, Adam's soul (humanity) evolved through five phases: Zero (still) through Four (spiritual).

When each phase arises, humanity experiences it to the fullest until it exhausts itself. Then, the next level of desire appears according to the sequence of *Reshimot* embedded in us. Until today, we had already experienced all the *Reshimot* of all the desires from Still to Speaking. All that's left for the evolution of humanity to be complete is to experience the spiritual desires to the fullest. Then, our unity with the Creator will be achieved.

Actually, the appearance of desires at the fifth level—the spiritual—began back in the 16th century, as was described by the Holy Ari. But today we are witnessing the appearance of the most intense kind within the fifth level—the spiritual *within* the spiritual. Moreover, we are witnessing its appearance in huge numbers, with millions of people the world over seeking spiritual answers to their questions.

Because the *Reshimot* that surface today are of greater desires for spirituality than ever before, the primary questions people are asking are about their origins, their roots! Although most of these seekers have a roof over their heads and sufficient income to support themselves and their families, they need to know where they came from, by whose plan, and for what purpose. When they are not satisfied with the answers religions offer, they seek them in other disciplines and teachings.

PHASE FOUR –
THE PHASE OF CONSCIOUS EVOLUTION

The main difference between Phase Four and all other phases is that in this phase, we must *consciously* evolve. In previous phases, it was always Nature that compelled us to move from one phase to the next. It did this by pressuring us enough to feel uncomfortable and seek to change our present state. This is how Nature develops all of its parts: human, animate, vegetative, and even inanimate.

Our basic desire is passive. This is because we are meant to be receivers of pleasure, not givers of it (except in our intention). Hence, we only move from one state to the next when pressure becomes intolerable. Otherwise, we prefer to stay motionless. The logic is simple: If I am fine where I am, why move?

But Nature has a different plan in store for us. Instead of allowing us to remain complacent in our present state, it wants us to evolve until we reach its own level, the level of the Creator. This, after all, is the purpose of Creation.

So we have two options: we can choose to evolve through Nature's pressure, which might be unpleasant, or we can evolve painlessly by becoming active in developing our awareness. Remaining passive and undeveloped is not an option because it doesn't fit into Nature's plan when it created us.

When our spiritual level begins to evolve, it can only happen if we *want* it to evolve so we can reach the same condition as the Creator's. Just as in Phase Four in the Four Phases, we are now required to *voluntarily* change our desire.

Therefore, Nature will continue pressuring us. We will continue to be struck by hurricanes, earthquakes, epidemics, terrorism, and all kinds of natural and man-made hardships until we realize that we *have* to change, that we must consciously return to our Root.

As we have said, the physical world was created when the soul of *Adam ha Rishon* shattered. In that state, all the desires began to appear one by one from light to heavy, from still to spiritual, creating our world phase by phase.

Today, at the beginning of the 21st century, all the degrees have already been completed except for the desire for spirituality, which is surfacing now. When we correct it, we will unite with the Creator because our desire for spirituality is actually the desire for unity with Him. This will be the apex of the evolutionary process of the world and of humanity.

By consciously increasing our desire to return to our spiritual root, we build a spiritual *Kli*. The Surrounding Light corrects the *Kli* and develops it. Each new level of development evokes a new *Reshimo*, a record of a past state that we had already experienced when we were more corrected. Eventually, the Surrounding Light corrects the whole *Kli*, and the soul of *Adam ha Rishon* is reunited with all its parts and with the Creator.

But this process leads to a question: if the *Reshimot* are recorded within me, and if the states are evoked and experienced within me, too, then where is the objective reality in all of this? If another person has different *Reshimot*, does that mean that he or she is living in a different world than mine? And what about the spiritual worlds, where do they exist if everything I experience exists only within me? Moreover, where is the "Creator's home"?

Part Three will try to answer all these questions.

PART THREE

Talk about Reality

5
ALL IN ONE AND ONE IN ALL

*"We see a great world before us, and all the wondrous
things it contains. But in fact, we see all that, only
within us. In other words, there is a kind of photographic
machine in the back of our brain, which portrays everything that we see, and there is nothing outside of us!"*

~Baal HaSulam,
"Preface to the Book of Zohar"

Of all the unexpected concepts found in Kabbalah, there
is none so unpredictable, unreasonable, yet so profound
and fascinating as the concept of reality. Had it not been
for Einstein and the subsequent quantum physicists, who
revolutionized the way we think about reality, the ideas
presented here would have been brushed off as absurd.

93

In the previous chapter, we said that evolution unfolds as a manifestation of our growing egoistic desires. But if our desires propel the evolution of our world, what would happen if we had no desires at all? Would there still be a world? Because if desires propel evolution, perhaps our world is just a figment of our desires, a tale we *want* to believe?

In Chapter Three, we said that Creation started from the Thought of Creation, which created the Four Basic Phases of Light. These Phases include ten *Sefirot*: *Keter* (the Root Phase), *Hochma* (Phase One), *Bina* (Phase Two), *Hesed*, *Gevura*, *Tifferet*, *Netzah*, *Hod*, and *Yesod* (all of which comprise Phase Three—*Zeir Anpin*), and *Malchut* (Phase Four). *The Book of Zohar* states that the whole of reality consists of only ten *Sefirot*, or the four basic phases (Figure 9).

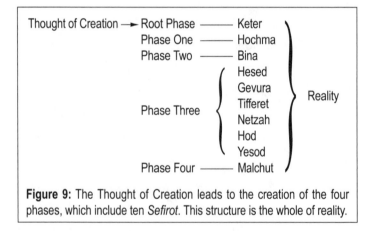

Figure 9: The Thought of Creation leads to the creation of the four phases, which include ten *Sefirot*. This structure is the whole of reality.

Just as atoms are the building blocks of our world, the ten-*Sefirot* structure is the building block of the spiritual worlds. Both are made of "positive," giving parts, which include the *Sefirot* from *Keter* to *Yesod*, and a "negative," receiving part, *Malchut*. This is the basic, indivisible structure of the spiritual reality.

In the previous chapter we said that "the only difference between people is in the way they want to experience pleasure," in their desires. Thus, our different desires create a different reality for each of us, though all of our "realities" consist of the same basic substance: a desire to experience pleasure.

When we use our corporeal, egoistic desires to experience reality, we call what we experience "our world." And when we experience the ten-*Sefirot* structure with our spiritual desires, we call it "the spiritual world." Spiritual desires also have a different name, *Kelim* (vessels).

And just as we need senses to perceive the physical reality, we need vessels to perceive the spiritual reality. The purpose of the wisdom of Kabbalah is to help us develop those vessels. As our brains use the letters of the alphabet to study and describe this world, our spiritual vessels use the ten-*Sefirot* structure to study and describe the spiritual worlds.

And lastly, to understand this world, we must follow certain restrictions and rules of study and experimentation. Similarly, to achieve the most accurate understanding of spirituality, we need to know which rules and restrictions to follow in the spiritual worlds.

THREE BOUNDARIES IN STUDYING THE UPPER WORLDS

The spiritual worlds have three boundaries, or guidelines. To achieve the Purpose of Creation and become like the Creator, we need only follow them.

A Kabbalist's advice

Kabbalists' tips are never forceful or coercive. They suggest, but it is we who must choose whether or not to follow their advice. In the "Preface to the Book of Zohar," Baal HaSulam introduces three boundaries. He explains that following them is the easiest and fastest way to achieve spirituality. He also says that these guidelines are the only way to study Kabbalah in a way that will grant the student spiritual perception. But Baal HaSulam also says there are other ways to study; and although he warns that they are spiritually futile, the option of trying them out is open to anyone.

FIRST BOUNDARY – WHAT WE PERCEIVE

In his "Preface to The Book of Zohar," Baal HaSulam writes that there are "four categories of perception—Matter, Form in Matter, Abstract Form, and Essence." When we research the spiritual Nature, we should only work with those categories that yield solid, reliable information.

As we will soon see, only the first two categories, Matter and Form in Matter, are workable for us. This is why *The Book of Zohar* explains only those two, and every word in it is written either from the perspectives of Matter or Form in Matter. There is not a single word in it from the perspectives of Abstract Form or Essence.

SECOND BOUNDARY — WHERE WE PERCEIVE

As we've said before, we are all pieces of the soul of *Adam ha Rishon*, which was initially created in the Upper Worlds and then broke in pieces. *The Zohar* teaches that the vast majority of the pieces, ninety-nine percent to be exact, were scattered in the worlds *Beria*, *Yetzira*, and *Assiya* (BYA), and the remaining one percent rose to *Atzilut*.

Thus, Adam's scattered soul makes up the content of the worlds BYA. And since we are all pieces of that soul, clearly everything we perceive can only be parts of these worlds. So even when we achieve spirituality, everything we sense as coming from higher worlds than BYA, such as *Atzilut* or *Adam Kadmon*, is inaccurate whether or not it appears that way to us. All we can perceive of the worlds *Atzilut* and *Adam Kadmon* are reflections, seen through the filters of the worlds BYA.

Our world is at the lowest degree of the worlds BYA. In fact, the degree called "our world" is completely opposite in nature from the spiritual worlds. This is why we don't feel them in our world. It is as if two people were standing back to back and going in opposite directions. What are their chances of ever meeting each other?

But when we correct ourselves, we "open our eyes" and discover that we are already living in the worlds BYA.

Eventually, we will even rise along with them to *Atzilut* and to *Adam Kadmon*.

THIRD BOUNDARY – WHO PERCEIVES

Even though *The Zohar* describes the content of each world and what happens there in great detail, almost as if there were a physical place where these processes unfold, it refers only to the experiences of souls. In other words, it relates to how Kabbalists *perceive* things, and tells us about them so that we, too, can experience them. Therefore, when we read in *The Zohar* about events in the worlds *BYA*, we are actually learning how Rabbi Shimon Bar-Yochai (Rashbi), author of *The Book of Zohar*, perceived spiritual states.

Also, when Kabbalists write about the worlds above *BYA*, they are not actually writing about those higher worlds, but about how *the writers* perceived those worlds while being in the worlds *BYA*. And because Kabbalists write about their personal experiences, there are similarities and differences in Kabbalistic writings.

Some of what they write relates to the general structure of the worlds, such as the names of the *Sefirot* and the worlds. This is especially true for Kabbalist teachers such as Baal HaSulam and the Ari. Other writings relate to personal experiences of Kabbalists in these worlds.

For example, if I tell a friend about my trip to New York, I might talk about Times Square or the great bridges that connect Manhattan to the mainland. But I might also talk about how overwhelmed I felt driving across the massive Brooklyn Bridge, and what it feels like to stand in the middle of Times Square, engulfed in the dazzling display of light, color, and sound, enveloped by a sense of total anonymity.

The difference between the first two examples and the latter two is that in the latter pair I am reporting personal experiences. In the first two, I am speaking of impressions that everyone will have while in Manhattan, though everyone will experience them differently.

The Book of Zohar shouldn't be treated like a report of mystical events or a collection of tales. Like all Kabbalah books, *The Zohar* should be used as a learning tool. This means that the book will help you only if you want to experience what it describes. Otherwise, the book will be of little help to you, and you will not understand it.

Understanding Kabbalistic texts correctly depends on your *intention* while reading them, on the reason why you opened them, *not* on your intellectual abilities. Only if you want to be transformed into the altruistic qualities that the text describes will the book affect you.

When we talked about the First Boundary, we said that *The Book of Zohar* speaks only from the perspectives of Matter and Form in Matter. Baal HaSulam explains that the Matter that *The Book of Zohar* describes is the will to receive, and the Form in Matter is the intention with which the will to receive operates—for me or for others.

In simpler terms: Matter = will to receive; Form = intention.

The Form of bestowal in and of itself is called "the world *Atzilut.*" Bestowal in its Abstract Form is the attribute of the Creator; it is totally unrelated to the creatures that receive it by their nature. However, the creatures (people) *can* wrap their will to receive with the *Form* of bestowal, so it is turned into bestowal. In other words, we can receive, and in so doing actually become givers.

There are two reasons why we cannot simply give:

1) To give, there must be someone who wants to receive. But besides us (the souls), there is only the Creator, who doesn't need to receive anything, since His nature is giving. Therefore, giving is not a viable option for us.

2) Because the Creator wants to give, He originally created only with a desire to receive. Reception is our substance, our Matter.

Now, this latter reason is more complex than it may seem at first. When Kabbalists write that all we want is to receive, they don't mean that all we *do* is receive, but that this is the underlying motivation behind everything we do. They phrase it very plainly: If it doesn't give us pleasure, we can't do it. It's not only that we don't want to; we literally can't.

This is because The Creator (Nature, The Giving Force) created us with only a will to receive, since He only wants to give. Therefore, we need not change our actions, but only the underlying motivation behind them.

PERCEIVING REALITY
CORRECTLY

Many terms are used to describe "understanding." For Kabbalists, the deepest level of understanding is called "attainment." Since they are studying the spiritual worlds, their goal is to reach "spiritual attainment." Attainment refers to such profound and thorough understanding and perception, no questions remain unanswered. Kabbalists write that at the end of humanity's evolution, we will all attain the Creator in a state called "Equivalence of Form."

To reach that goal, Kabbalists carefully defined which parts of reality we should study, and which we shouldn't. To determine these two paths, Kabbalists followed a very simple principle: If what we study helps us learn more quickly and more accurately, we should study it. If it doesn't, we should ignore it.

Therefore, Kabbalists in general, and *The Book of Zohar* in particular, caution us to study only what we can perceive with absolute certainty. Wherever guesswork is involved, we shouldn't waste our time, as our attainment would be questionable.

Kabbalists also say that of the four categories of perception—Matter, Form in Matter, Abstract Form, and Essence—we can perceive only the first two with certainty. Thus, everything *The Zohar* writes about is desires (Matter) and how we use them: for ourselves or for the Creator (Form in Matter).

Kabbalist Yehuda Ashlag writes that, "If the reader does not know how to be prudent with the boundaries, and takes matters out of context, he or she will immediately be confused." This can happen if we don't limit our study to Matter and Form in Matter.

There is no such thing as a "prohibition" in spirituality. When Kabbalists declare something as "forbidden," it means that it is unattainable, imperceptible. When they say that we are forbidden to study Abstract Form and Essence, it doesn't mean that we'll be struck by lightning if we do; it means that we can't hope to achieve clear perception of them, even if we really want to.

Ashlag uses electricity to explain why the Essence is imperceptible. He says that we can use electricity in many different ways, such as heating, cooling, playing music, and watching videos. Electricity can be dressed in many Forms; but can we express the Essence of electricity itself?

Let's use another example to explain the four categories—Matter, Form in Matter, Abstract Form, and Essence. When we say that a certain person is strong, we are actually referring to that person's Matter—body—and the Form that clothes his or her Matter—strength.

If we remove the Form of strength from the Matter (the person's body), and examine the Form of strength separately, undressed in Matter, we would be examining the Abstract Form of strength.

The fourth category, the Essence of the person in itself, is completely unattainable. We simply have no senses that can "study" the Essence and portray it in a perceptible manner. In consequence, the Essence is not only something we don't know right now; we will *never* know it.

The Confusion Trap

Why should we focus on only the first two categories? The problem is that when dealing with spirituality, we don't know when we are confused. Therefore, we might well continue in the wrong direction and drift farther away from the truth.

In the material world, if I know what I want, I can see if I'm getting it or not, or at least if I'm on the right track toward getting it. Unfortunately, this is not the case with spirituality. In that arena, when I am wrong, I am not only denied what I wanted, but I even lose my present spiritual degree. The Light will dim and I will be unable to redirect myself correctly without help from a guide. This is why it is so important to understand the three boundaries and follow them.

A NONEXISTENT REALITY

Now that we understand what we can study and what we can't, let's see what we are actually studying and perceiving through our senses. Baal HaSulam, who researched the whole of reality and then wrote about his discoveries, said that we do not and can not know what exists outside of us. For example, we have no idea what is outside our ears, what makes our eardrums respond. All we know is that our ears are reacting to a stimulus from the outside.

Even the names we attach to phenomena have nothing to do with the phenomena themselves, but with our reactions to them. At any given moment, numerous events happen right next to us, but we are unaware of them. They go unnoticed by our senses because we relate only to phenomena that our senses can perceive. This is why we can't perceive the Essence of anything outside of us: we only study our reactions to events and to objects, not to the events and the objects themselves.

This rule of perception applies not only to the spiritual worlds; it's the law of the whole of Nature. Relating to reality in this way immediately makes us realize that what we see is not what actually exists. This understanding is paramount if we want to achieve spiritual progress.

To relate correctly to reality, we mustn't think that what we are perceiving is the "real" picture. In other words, the fact that we see a red apple as red doesn't mean that it is actually red, only that I am *perceiving* it as red.

Actually, if you ask physicists, they'll tell you that the only true statement you can make about a red apple is that it's *not* red. If you remember how the *Masach* (Screen) works, you know that it receives what it can receive in order to give to the Creator, and rejects the rest.

Similarly, an object's color is determined by light waves that the illuminated object *couldn't* absorb. We are not seeing the color of the object itself, but the light that the object *rejected*. The real color of the object is the light that it absorbed; but because it absorbed this light, it cannot reach our eye, and we therefore can't see it. This is why the red apple's real color is anything but red.

Here's how Baal HaSulam, in the "Preface to The Book of Zohar," relates to our lack of perception of the Essence: "It is known that what we cannot feel, we also cannot imagine; and what we cannot sense, we cannot imagine, either. ... It follows that the thought has no perception of the Essence whatsoever."

In other words, because we cannot sense an Essence, any Essence, we also cannot perceive it. But the concept that baffles most Kabbalah students the first time they study Baal HaSulam's Preface is how little we really know about *ourselves*. Here's what he has written in this regard: "Moreover, we do not even know our own Essence. I feel and know that I occupy a certain space in the world, that I am solid, warm, and that I think, and other such manifestations of the operations of my Essence. Yet, if you ask me what is my own Essence ... I will not know what to answer you."

THE MEASUREMENT MECHANISM

Let's look at our perception problem from a more mechanical angle. Our senses are instruments that measure everything they perceive. When we hear a sound, we determine if it's loud or soft; when we see an object, we can (usually) tell which color it is; and when we touch something, we immediately know if it's warm or cool, wet or dry.

All measurement tools operate similarly. Think of a scale with a one-pound weight on it. The traditional weighing mechanism is made of a spring that stretches according to the weight, and a ruler that measures the tightness of the spring. Once the spring stops stretching and rests at a certain point, the numbers on the ruler indicate the weight. Actually, we are not measuring the weight, but the balance between the spring and the weight (Figure 10).

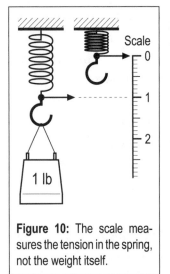

Figure 10: The scale measures the tension in the spring, not the weight itself.

This is why Baal Ha-Sulam says that we cannot perceive the Abstract Form, the object in and of itself, because we have absolutely no connection with it. If we can place the object on a spring and measure how it stretches the spring, we'll get a result. But if we can't measure what is happening on the outside, if we have no perception of the external object, it's as though there is no object at all. Moreover, if we use a defective spring to measure an external object, we will get the wrong result. This is what happens when we grow older and our senses begin to deteriorate.

In spiritual terms, the outside world presents Abstract Forms to us, such as the weight. Using the spring and the dial—the will to receive and the intention to bestow—we measure how much of the Abstract Form we can receive. If we could build a gauge that would "measure" the Creator, we could sense Him just as we sense this world.

In fact, there is such a gauge—it is known as "the sixth sense."

THE SIXTH SENSE

Let's begin this section with a little fantasy: You are in a dark space, a complete void. You cannot see a thing; you cannot hear a sound, there are no smells and no flavors, and there is nothing you can touch around you. Now imagine being in this state for such a long time that you forgot you ever had senses that could feel such things. Eventually, you even forgot that such sensations could exist.

All of a sudden, a faint aroma appears. It grows stronger, surrounds you, but you can't pinpoint its location. Then, more fragrances appear, some strong, some weak, some sweet and some sour. Using them, you can now find your way in the world. Different aromas come from different places, and you can begin to find your way by following them.

Then, without forewarning, sounds appear from all around you. There are many kinds of sounds; some like music, some like words, and some are simply noise. But the sounds provide additional orientation in that space.

Now you can measure distances, directions; you can guess the sources of the smells and the sounds you are receiving. This is no longer just a space you're in; it's a whole world of sounds and scents.

After some time, a new revelation is made when something touches you. Shortly after, you discover more things you can touch. Some are cold, some are warm, some are dry, and some are moist. Some are hard and some are soft; some you can't decide which they are. You discover that you can put some of these objects in your mouth, and that they have distinct flavors.

By now you are living in a plentiful world of sounds, smells, sensations, and flavors. You can touch the objects in your world, and you can study your environment.

This is the world of the blind-from-birth. If you were in their shoes, would you feel that you needed the sense of sight? Would you even know that you don't have it? Never, unless someone told you about it or you'd had it before.

The same is true for the sixth sense. Without Kabbalah books, we'd never know we had once had it. Although we don't remember having this sense, we all had it prior to the breaking of *Adam ha Rishon*, of which we are all parts.

The sixth sense operates much like the five natural senses. The only difference is that the sixth sense is not given by nature; we have to develop and cultivate it. In fact, the name "sixth sense" is a bit misleading because we are not actually developing another sense; we are developing an *intention*, a new approach to our perception of reality.

While developing this intention, we study the Creator's Forms, the Forms of Bestowal, opposite from our natural egoistic makeup. This is why the sixth sense is not given to us by Nature; it is opposite from us.

Building the intention over each desire we feel is what makes us conscious of who we are, who the Creator is, and whether or not we want to be like Him. Only if we have two options before us can we make a true choice. Therefore, the Creator does not force us to be altruistic, like Him, but shows us who we are, who He is, and lets us make our own free choice. Once we've made our choice, we become the people we intend to be: Creator-like, or not.

Why, then, do we call the intention to bestow "the sixth sense"? The answer is simple: by having the same intention as the Creator, we become Creator-like. This means that we not only have the same intention, but because we have developed equivalence of form with Him, we see and perceive things we would not perceive otherwise. We actually begin to see through His eyes!

CREATE YOUR PERFECT REALITY

In Chapter Three, we explained the making of the *Kli* through the Creator's Light. In fact, of the two, the *Kli* is more important to us than the Light, even though obtaining the latter is our actual goal.

Let's clarify this with an example. In the film, *What the Bleep Do We Know!?* Dr. Candace Pert explains that if a certain Form does not exist within me in advance, I will not be able to see it on the outside. As an example, she uses a story about how the Indians first discovered Columbus' ships. She says that it is commonly believed that when the ships arrived, the Indians could not see them, even though they were looking straight at them.

Dr. Pert explains that the Indians couldn't see the ships because they didn't have a model of such ships in their minds *before* they encountered them. Only the shaman, who was curious about the odd ripples that seemed to come from nowhere, discovered the ships after trying to imagine what could be causing the ripples. His imagination created various shapes in his mind, and when the shape in his mind resembled that of the ships, he discovered them. At that point, he told his tribesmen what he saw, and then they, too, could see the ships.

Kabbalistically speaking, it takes an inner *Kli* to detect an outer object. In fact, the *Kelim* (plural for *Kli*) not only detect the outer reality, they create it! Thus, Columbus' armada existed only in the minds, the inner *Kelim* of the Indians who saw it and reported it.

There is no such thing as an "outside world." There are desires, *Kelim*, that create the outside world according to their own shapes. Outside us there is only Abstract Form, the intangible, imperceptible Creator. We shape our world by shaping our own tools of perception, our own *Kelim*.

If a tree falls in a forest, and nobody's around to hear it, does it still make a sound?

This famous Zen koan (a special kind of Zen riddle) can also be phrased in Kabbalistic terms: If there is no *Kli* that detects the sound of the tree, how can we know that it made a sound at all? Similarly, we could turn Columbus' discovery into a Zen koan and ask, "Before Columbus discovered America, did it exist?"

Therefore, it will not help us to ask the Creator to change the world around us for the better. The world is neither good nor bad; it's a reflection of the state of our own *Kelim*. When we correct our *Kelim* and make them beautiful, the world will be beautiful, as well. The *Tikkun* (correction) is within, and so is the Creator. He is our corrected selves.

Similarly, to a night owl, a night in the dark forest is the time of best visibility. To us, it is a time of chilling blindness. Our reality is but a projection of our inner *Kelim*, and what we call "the real world" is only a reflection of our inner correction or corruption. We are actually living in an imaginary world.

If we are to rise above this imaginary world to the real world, to the true perception, we must adapt ourselves to the true *Kelim*. At the end of the day, whatever we perceive will be according to our inner makeup, according to the way we build these models within us. There is nothing to discover outside of us, nothing to reveal except the abstract Upper Light that operates on us and reveals the new images within us, depending on our readiness to accept them.

Now all that remains is to learn where we can find the corrected *Kelim*. Do they exist within us or do we have to build them? And if we have to build them, how do we go about it? This will be the topic of the following sections.

THE THOUGHT OF CREATION

Kelim are the building blocks of the soul. The desires are the building materials, the bricks and the wood; our intentions are our tools, our screwdrivers, drills, and hammers.

But as with building a house, we need to read the blueprint before we can begin the work. Unfortunately, the Creator, or Architect of the blueprint is reluctant to give it to us. Instead, he wants us to study and execute the Master Plan of our souls independently. Only in this way can we ever really understand His Thought and become like Him.

To learn who He is, we must attentively watch what He does and come to understand Him through His actions. Kabbalists phrase it very succinctly: "By Your actions, we know You."

Our desires, the souls' raw materials, already exist. He gave them to us, and we just have to learn how to use them correctly and place the right intentions on them. Then, our souls will be corrected.

But as we have said before, the right intentions are altruistic intentions. In other words, we need to want our desires to be used to benefit others, not ourselves. By doing so, we will actually be benefiting ourselves, since we are all parts of the soul of *Adam ha Rishon*. Whether we like it or not, harming others comes back to us like a boomerang returns to its thrower, and just as forcefully.

Let's recap for a moment. A corrected *Kli* is a desire used with altruistic intentions. And conversely, a corrupted *Kli* is a desire used with egoistic intentions. By using a *Kli* altruistically, we use a desire in the same way the Creator does, and thus equalize with Him, at least concerning that specific desire. This is how we study His Thought.

Our only problem is to change the intentions with which we use our desires. But for that to happen we must see at least one other way of using them. We need an example of what other intentions look or feel like so we can decide whether we want them or not. When we see no other way of using our desires, we're trapped in the ones we already have. In that state, how can we find other intentions? Is this a trap or are we missing something? The next section will answer that.

BACK TO THE FUTURE

Kabbalists explain that thinking we are missing something is indeed a trap, but it's not a deadlock. If we follow the path of our *Reshimot*, an example of another intention will appear by itself. So let's reexamine the concept of *Reshimot*, and see how they can help us out of the trap.

Reshimot, as we stated in Chapter Four, are records, recollections of past states. Each *Reshimo* that a soul experiences along its spiritual path is collected in a special "data bank."

When we want to climb up the spiritual ladder, these *Reshimot* comprise our trail. They resurface one at a time, and we relive them. The faster we re-experience each *Reshimo*, the faster we exhaust it and move on to the next recollection.

The next *Reshimo* is the state that created our present state as they cascaded from the four basic phases, through the worlds ABYA and down to our world. Because now we are climbing back up the ladder, the next *Reshimo* is the progenitor of the present state, and is therefore higher than the present state.

We must always remember that our spiritual roots are *above*, not below. Returning to the roots means climbing, not digging down. This is why a climb is a return to the roots, and why the *Reshimot* that appear during that climb are always higher spiritual states. The reason we don't experience them as higher testifies to our own corruption, not to the actual degree of the *Reshimot* we are experiencing.

TWO APPROACHES, TWO PATHS

We cannot change the order of the *Reshimot*. That has already been determined on our way down. But we can and should determine what we will do with each of them. If we are passive and simply wait for the *Reshimot* to change, it will take a long time before we thoroughly experience them, and before that happens they can cause us great pain. This is why the passive approach is called "the path of pain."

On the other hand, we can take an active approach by trying to relate to each *Reshimo* as to "another day in school," seeking to understand what the Creator is trying to teach us. If we simply remember that this world is our practice field, we will tremendously speed up the passing of the *Reshimot*. This active approach is called "the path of Light," because our efforts connect us to the Creator, to the Light, instead of to our present state, as is the case with the passive approach.

Actually, our efforts don't have to succeed; trying is what matters. By increasing our desires to be like the Creator (altruistic), we attach ourselves to higher, more spiritual states.

DESIRE MAKES FOR PROGRESS

The process of spiritual progress is very similar to the way children learn; it is basically a process of imitation. By imitating grownups, even though they don't know what they are doing, they create within themselves the *desire* to learn.

Note: It's not what children know that promotes their growth; it's the simple fact that they *want to know.* The desire to know is enough to evoke in them the next *Reshimo*, the one in which they already know.

Because the *Reshimot* are connected in a chain, when the present *Reshimo* exhausts itself and leaves, it "pulls in" the next *Reshimo* in line. Thus, we are not really learning anything new in this world or in the spiritual world; we are simply climbing "back to the future."

If we want to be more giving, like the Creator, we should constantly examine ourselves and see if we fit the description that we consider spiritual (altruistic). In this way, our desire to be more altruistic will help us develop a more accurate, detailed perception of ourselves compared to the Creator.

If we do not want to be egoistic, our desires will evoke the *Reshimot* that will show us what being more altruistic means. Every time we decide that we do not want to use this or that desire egoistically, the *Reshimo* of that state is considered to have completed its task, and moves on to make room for the next. This is the only correction we are required to make.

In his book, *Shamati (I Heard)*, Baal HaSulam phrases this principle in these words: "...where by hating the evil [egoism] in earnest truth it is corrected." And then he explains: "...if two people come to realize that each hates what one's friend hates, and loves what and whom one's friend loves, they come into perpetual bonding, as a stake that will never fall. Hence, since the Creator loves to bestow, the lower ones should also adapt to want only to bestow. The Creator also hates to be a receiver, as He is completely whole and needs nothing. Thus, man too must hate the matter of reception for oneself. It follows from all the above that one must hate the will to receive bitterly, for all the ruins in the world come only from the will to receive. Through the hatred one corrects it."

Thus, simply by wanting it, we evoke *Reshimot* of more altruistic desires, which already existed within us from the time we were connected in the soul of *Adam ha Rishon*. These *Reshimot* correct us and make us more like our Creator. Therefore, desire (the *Kli*) is both the engine of change and the means for correction. We need not suppress our desires. We simply need to learn how to work with them productively for ourselves and others.

PART FOUR

Crisis and Correction

Before we talk about how Kabbalistic concepts can help us in our day-to-day lives, let's see what we've learned so far. It might come as a surprise, but you already know quite a bit about Kabbalah. You know that Kabbalah started about 5,000 years ago in Mesopotamia (today's Iraq), when people were searching for the purpose of their lives. Those people, led by Abraham the Patriarch, discovered that the reason we are all born is to receive the ultimate pleasure of becoming like the Creator. When they discovered it, they built study groups and began to spread the word.

Those first Kabbalists told us that all we're made of is a will to receive pleasure, which they separated into five levels—still, vegetative, animate, speaking, and spiritual. The will to receive is very important because it's the engine behind everything we do in this world. In other words, we're always trying to receive pleasure, and the more we have, the more we want. As a result, we're always evolving and changing.

Later, we learned that Creation was formed in a four-phase process, where the Root (0), which is synonymous with the Light and the Creator, created the will to receive (1); the will to receive then wanted to give (2), then decided to receive as a way of giving (3), and finally wanted to receive once more (4). But this time it wanted to receive the knowledge of how to be the Creator, the *Giver*.

After the four phases and their Root, the will to receive was divided into five worlds—*Adam Kadmon, Atzilut, Beria, Yetzira,* and *Assiya*—and one soul, called *Adam ha Rishon. Adam ha Rishon* broke and materialized in our world. In other words, all of us are actually one soul, whose parts are connected and dependent on each other like cells in a body.

But when the will to receive grew, we became more self-centered and stopped feeling that we were one. Instead, today we only feel ourselves, and even if we do relate to others it is done to receive pleasure through them.

This egoistic state is called "the broken soul of *Adam ha Rishon,*" and it is our task, as parts of that soul, to correct it. Actually, we don't have to correct it, but we must be aware that we are broken and want to become corrected. When we realize that, we will begin to look for a way out of the trap of this law, the egoism trap.

Looking for freedom from the ego leads to the emergence of the "point in the heart," the desire for spirituality. The "point in the heart" is like any desire; it increases and decreases through the influence of the environment. If we want to increase our desire for spirituality, we need to build an environment that promotes it. In this section, we will talk about what needs to be done to have an environment that is spiritually supportive on personal, social, and international levels.

6
A New Method for a New Desire

THE DARK
BEFORE THE DAWN

The darkest time of night is right before the dawn. Similarly, the writers of *The Book of Zohar* said, almost 2,000 years ago, that humanity's darkest time will come right before its spiritual awakening. For centuries, beginning with the Ari, who lived in the 16th century, Kabbalists have been writing that the time *The Book of Zohar* referred to was the end of the 20th century. They called it "the last generation."

They did not mean that we would all perish in some apocalyptic, spectacular event. In Kabbalah, a generation represents a spiritual state. The last generation is the last and *highest* state that can be reached. And Kabbalists said that the time we are living in—the beginning of the 21ˢᵗ century—is when we would see the generation of the spiritual ascent, the last state of our evolution.

But these Kabbalists also said that for this change to happen, we must change the way we are evolving. They said that today, a conscious, voluntary evolution is required, born of our own free choice to grow.

As with any beginning or birth, the emergence of the last generation, the generation of free choice, is no easy process. Until recently, we have been evolving in our lower desires—still through speaking—leaving out the spiritual level. But now the spiritual *Reshimot* are surfacing in millions of people, demanding that we realize them.

When these *Reshimot* first appear in us, we still lack the appropriate method to deal with them. They are like a whole new technology that we must learn how to work with. So while we are still learning, we try to realize the new kind of *Reshimot* with our old ways of thought, because those ways helped us realize our lower level *Reshimot*. But those ways are inadequate for handling the new *Reshimot*, and therefore fail to do their job, and live us empty and frustrated.

When spiritual *Reshimot* surface in an individual, without the method to satisfy them, frustration arises, then depression, until one learns how to relate to these new desires. This usually happens by applying the wisdom of Kabbalah, which was originally designed to cope with spiritual *Reshimot*, as we've described in Chapter One.

If, however, one cannot find the solution, the individual might plunge into workaholism, addictions of all kinds, and other attempts to suppress the problem of the new desires, trying to avoid coping with an incurable ache.

On a personal level, such a state is very distressing but it doesn't pose a problem serious enough to destabilize the social structure. However, when spiritual *Reshimot* appear in millions of people at approximately the same time, and particularly if this happens in many countries simultaneously, you have a global crisis on your hands. And a global crisis calls for a global solution.

Today, it is no secret that humanity is in a global crisis. Depression is soaring to unprecedented rates in the United States, but the picture isn't much brighter in other developed countries. In 2001, the World Health Organization (WHO) reported that "depression is the leading cause of disability in the U.S. and worldwide."

Another major problem in modern society is the alarming abundance of drug abuse. Drugs have always been in use, but in the past they were used primarily for medicine and rituals, while today they are being used at a much earlier age, primarily to alleviate the emotional void that so many young people feel. And because depression is soaring, so is the use of drugs and drug-related crimes.

Another facet of the crisis is the state of the family unit. The family institution used to be an icon of stability, warmth, and shelter, but not any more. According to the National Center for Health Statistics, for every two couples that marry, one divorces, and the figures are similar throughout the Western world.

Moreover, couples no longer must go through a major crisis or personality clash to decide on a divorce. Today, even couples in their 50s and 60s separate once their kids have left home. Since their incomes are secured, they're not afraid of starting a new chapter at ages that only a few years back were considered unacceptable for such steps.

We even have a phrase that spares us facing this painful aspect of our social crisis: "the empty nest syndrome." Yet, the bottom line is that people divorce because once their children have left home, there is nothing to keep them together, since there is simply no love between them.

It was therefore not surprising to read these words on *The New York Times* October 15, 2006 edition: "Married couples, whose numbers have been declining for decades as a proportion of American households, have finally slipped into a minority, according to an analysis of new census figures."

At the end of the day, it is not the financial stability that sets us apart, it is the simple fact that people don't love each other, only themselves. But if we remember that we were all deliberately created egoists by a force that wants to give, we might have a fighting chance. At least then we will know that we will not find the solution in ourselves, but in Him.

The crisis is unique not only in its universality, but in its versatility. This makes it much more comprehensive and difficult to handle. The crisis is happening in just about every field of human engagement—personal, social, international, in science, medicine, and the environment. For example, until just a few years ago, "the weather" was simply a convenient haven when one had nothing to contribute about other topics. Today, however, we are required to be climate savvy. Hot topics nowadays are climate change, global warming, rising sea levels, and the start of the new hurricane season.

"The Big Thaw" is what Geoffrey Lean of *The Independent* ironically called the state of the planet in an online article published November 20, 2005. Here's the title of Lean's article: "The Big Thaw: Global Disaster Will Follow If the Ice Cap on Greenland Melts." And the subtitle, "Now scientists say it is vanishing far faster than even they expected."

And weather is not the only disaster lurking on the horizon. The June 22, 2006 issue of the magazine, "Nature," published a University of California study stating that the San Andreas Fault is now overdue for the "Big One." According to Yuri Fialko of Scripps Institution of Oceanography at the University of California, "the fault is a significant seismic hazard and is primed for another big earthquake."

And of course, if we survive the storms, the earthquakes, and the rising seas, there is always a Bin Laden in the area to remind us that our lives can be made significantly briefer than we had planned.

And finally, there are health issues that require our attention: AIDS, avian flu, mad cow disease, and of course, the old standbys: cancer, cardiovascular diseases, and diabetes await us. There are many more we can mention here, but by now you've probably gotten the point. While some of these health problems aren't new, they are mentioned here because they are spreading around the globe.

Conclusion: An ancient Chinese proverb says, "When you want to curse someone, tell him, 'May you live in interesting times.'" Our times are indeed interesting; but let's not consider this a curse. It is as *The Book of Zohar* promised—the darkness before the dawn. Now, let's talk about the solution.

A BRAVE NEW WORLD IN FOUR STEPS

It takes only four steps to change the world:
1. Acknowledge the existence of the crisis;
2. Expose its causes;
3. Determine the best solution;
4. Design a plan to resolve the crisis.

Let's examine them one at a time.

1. Acknowledge the existence of the crisis

Today, more than 130 countries participate in the Intergovernmental Panel on Climate Change (IPCC), and its reports clearly indicate that climate is changing for the worse. Yet, despite the accumulating evidence from all fields of science and society, many governments and international corporations still play down the gravity of the situation. Instead of being the first to tackle the issue, conflicting interests prevent them from cooperating to deal with the crisis effectively.

In addition, many people resist the idea that the world's problems are threatening their personal wellbeing. In consequence, they suppress the urgent need to deal with the problems, before they land at their doorsteps.

And the biggest of all problems is that we have no previous memory of living in such a precarious state. Because of that, we are unable to assess our situation correctly. That's not to say that catastrophes have never happened, but our time is unique in the sense that today catastrophes are happening on all fronts, instantaneously—in every aspect of human life, and all over the world.

2. Expose its causes

A crisis occurs when there's a collision between two elements, and the superior element forces its rule on the inferior one. Human nature, or egoism, is discovering how opposite it is from Nature, or altruism. This is why so many people feel distressed, depressed, insecure, and frustrated.

In short, the crisis isn't really happening on the outside, even though it certainly seems to take up physical space; it is happening within us. The crisis is the titanic clash between good (altruism) and evil (egoism). How sad it is that we have to play the bad guys in the real reality show. But don't lose hope—as in all shows, a happy end awaits.

3. Determine the best solution

The more we recognize the underlying cause of the crisis, our egoism, the more we will understand what needs to be changed in us and in our societies. By doing so, we will be able to de-escalate the crisis and bring society and ecology to a positive, constructive outcome. We will talk more about such changes as we explore the concept of freedom of choice.

4. Design a plan to resolve the crisis

Once we have completed the first three stages of the plan, we can draw it up in greater detail. But even the best plan needs the active support of leading, nationally recognized organizations to succeed. Therefore, the plan must have a broad base of international support from scientists, thinkers, politicians, and the United Nations, as well as the media and social organizations. The IPCC we mentioned in Item 1 of this list is a good example of such an entity.

Because we grow from one level of desire to the next, every time a crisis emerges, it should be treated as a new event. Our past experiences don't help us because past events happened at lower levels of desires. If our past experiences did help, we would not be talking about a crisis today.

Thus, everything that is happening now is happening for the first time on the spiritual level of desire. If we remember that, we can apply the knowledge of people who are connected to spirituality in the same way we have been applying scientific knowledge to cope with problems on the physical levels of desire.

Kabbalists, who have already made it to the spiritual worlds, the root of our world, see the *Reshimot* (spiritual roots) that are causing this state. They can guide us out of the maze we are in by looking at things from their source in the spiritual world. This support can help us resolve the crisis easily and quickly because we'll know why things happen and how we can best mend them.

Think of it this way: If you knew there were people who could predict the results of tomorrow's lottery, wouldn't you like them at your side when you're placing your bets?

There is no magic here, only knowledge of the rules of the game in the spiritual world. In the eyes of a Kabbalist, we're not in a crisis, we're just a little disoriented and hence keep betting on the wrong numbers. When we find our direction, resolving the (nonexistent) crisis will be a piece of cake, and so will be winning the lottery. And the beauty of Kabbalistic knowledge is that it has no copyrights; it belongs to everyone.

KNOW YOUR LIMITS

Lord, grant me strength to change what I can change, courage to accept what I cannot change, and the wisdom to discern between them.

~An Old Prayer

In our own eyes, we are unique and independently acting individuals. This is a common human trait. Just think of the centuries of battles humanity has been through, only to finally obtain the limited personal freedom we have today.

We are not the only ones who suffer when our freedom is taken. All creatures struggle when captured; it is an inherent, natural trait to object to any form of subjugation. But even if we understand that every creature deserves to be free, we do not necessarily understand what being free *really* means, or if and how it is connected to correcting humanity's egoism.

If we honestly ask ourselves about the meaning of freedom, we're likely to discover that our present concepts have changed by the time we're finished asking. So before we can talk about freedom, we must know what being free truly means.

To see if we understand freedom, we must look within ourselves to see if we are capable of even one free, voluntary act. Because our will to receive constantly grows, we are always urged to find better and more rewarding ways to live. Our growing desires leave us no choice in the matter.

On the other hand, if our will to receive is the cause of all this trouble, maybe there's a way to control it. If we could do so, perhaps we could control our lives. Otherwise, without this control, the decline seems unstoppable. In short, we seem to be trapped in a rat race against our own desires, and we appear to be losing.

Still, we go about our business as though events depend on our decisions. But do they really? Wouldn't it be better to give up trying to change our lives and just go with the flow?

On the one hand, we've just said that Nature objects to any subjugation. But on the other hand, Nature doesn't show us which, if any of our actions, is free, and where we are lured by an invisible Puppet Master into *thinking* we are free.

Moreover, if Nature has a plan for us, could these questions and uncertainties be part of the scheme? Perhaps there's an ulterior reason that makes us feel lost and confused? Maybe confusion and disillusionment are the Puppet Master's way of telling us, "Hey, take another look at where you're all going, because if you're looking for Me, you're looking in the wrong direction."

Few will deny that we are, indeed, disoriented. But to determine our direction we must know where to start looking. This can save us years of futile efforts. The first thing we want to discover is where we have free and independent choice, and where we don't. Once we realize this, we will know where we should focus our attention and our efforts.

THE REINS OF LIFE

The whole of Nature obeys only one law: "The Law of Pleasure and Pain." If the only substance in Creation is the will to receive pleasure, then only one rule of behavior is required: attraction to pleasure and rejection from pain.

Human beings are no exception to the rule. We follow a preinstalled design that entirely dictates our every move: we want to receive the most, for the least amount of work. And if possible, we want it all for free! Therefore, in

·

everything we do, even when we are unaware of it, we try to choose the pleasurable and avoid the painful.

Even when it seems we are sacrificing ourselves, we are actually receiving more pleasure from the "sacrifice" than from any other option we can conceive at that moment. And the reason we deceive ourselves into thinking we have altruistic motives is because deceiving ourselves is more fun than telling ourselves the truth. As writer Agnes Repplier once put it, "There are few nudities so objectionable as the naked truth."

Earlier, we said that Phase Two gives, even though it is actually motivated by the same will to receive as Phase One. This is the root of every "altruistic" action we "bestow" upon each other.

We see how everything we do follows a "calculation of profitability." For example, I calculate the price of an item compared to the prospective benefit from getting it. If I think that the pleasure (or lack of pain) from having the commodity will be greater than the price I must pay, I will tell my "inner broker, "Buy! Buy! Buy!" turning the lights green across my mental Wall Street board.

We can change our priorities, adopt different values of good and bad, and even "train" ourselves to become fearless. Moreover, we can make a goal so important in our eyes that any hardship involved in achieving it would become insignificant.

If, for example, I want the social status and good wages associated with being a famous physician, I will strain, sweat, and toil for years in medical school and live through several more years of sleep deprivation during internship, hoping it will eventually pay off in fame or fortune, or (preferably) both.

Sometimes the calculation of immediate pain for future gain is so natural, we don't even notice we are doing it. For example, if I became terribly ill and discovered that only a specific surgery could save my life, I would gladly have the operation. Although the operation itself might be very unpleasant and could pose risks of its own, it would be less threatening than my illness. I might even pay considerable sums to put myself through the ordeal.

CHANGING SOCIETY TO CHANGE MYSELF

Nature gave us three challenges: it "sentenced" us to constantly seek escape from suffering; it set us on a continuing pursuit of pleasure; and it denied us the ability to determine what kind of pleasure we really want. In other words, we can't control what we want. We are subject to a variety of desires that pop up within us, without asking our opinion in the matter.

Yet, Nature not only created our desires, it also provided us with a way to control them. If we remember that we are all parts of one soul, that of *Adam ha Rishon*, it will be easy to see that the way to control our own desires is to affect the whole soul, meaning humanity, or at least a part of it.

Let's look at it this way: If a single cell wanted to go left, but the rest of the body wanted to go right, the single cell would have to go right, too. That is, unless it convinced the whole body, or an overwhelming majority of the cells, or the body's "government," that it was better to go left.

So even though we can't control our own desires, *society* can and does control them. And because we can control our choice of society, we can choose the kind of society that will affect us as *we* think best. Put simply, we can use social influences to control our personal desires. And by controlling our desires, we'll control our thoughts and ultimately, our actions.

Almost two thousand years ago, *The Book of Zohar* had already described the importance of society. Since the 20th century, it has become evident that we depend on each other for physical survival. And now, with millions of people seeking spirituality, an effective use of our societal dependency has become vital for our spiritual progress. The paramount importance of society is a message that Baal HaSulam makes very clear in many of his essays.

Baal HaSulam says that every person's greatest wish, whether one admits it or not, is to be liked by others and to win their approval. This not only gives us a sense of confidence, but affirms our most precious possession—our ego. Without society's approval, we feel that our very existence is ignored and discarded. And because no ego can tolerate denial, people often go to extremes to win others' attention.

Because our greatest wish is to win society's approval, we are compelled to adapt to (and adopt) the laws of our environment. These laws determine not only our behavior, but design our attitudes and approaches to everything we do and think. For the most part, we don't feel that we are surrendering to society's rule, we simply devise new ideas that we think are our own. But we rarely stop to think where we got those ideas.

In such a situation, we are unable to make any free choices—from the way we live, to our interests, to how we spend our leisure, and even the food we eat and the clothes we wear. Even when we choose to dress contrary to fashion or regardless of it, we are still (trying to be) indifferent to a *certain social code* that we have chosen to ignore. In other words, if the fashion we choose to ignore hadn't existed, we wouldn't have had to ignore it and would probably have chosen a different dress code. Ultimately, the only way to change ourselves is to change the social norms of our environment. The next chapter will show how we can achieve that.

7
THE FOUR FACTORS
OF OUR MAKE-UP

If we are nothing more than products of our environment, and if there is no real freedom in what we do, think, or want, can we be held responsible for our actions? And if we are not responsible for them, who is?

To answer these questions we must first understand the four factors that comprise us, and how we can work with them to acquire freedom of choice. According to Kabbalah, we are controlled by four factors:

1) The Bed, also called First Matter
2) Unchanging Attributes of the Bed
3) Attributes that Change through External Forces
4) Changes in the External Environment.

Let's see what each of them means to us.

1. The Bed, the First Matter

Our unchanging essence is called "The Bed." I can be happy or sad, thoughtful, angry, alone or with others. In whatever mood and in whichever society, my basic *self* never changes.

To understand these four factors, let's look at the budding and dying of plants. Consider a stalk of wheat. When a wheat seed decays, it loses its form entirely. But even though it has completely lost its form, only a new stalk of wheat will emerge from that seed. This is because the bed of the wheat remains the same, and the essence of the seed is always that of wheat.

2. Unchanging Attributes of the Bed

Just as the bed is unchanging and wheat always produces new wheat, the way wheat seeds develop is also unchanging. A single stalk may produce more than one stalk in the new life cycle, and the quantity and quality of the new buds might change. Yet the bed itself, the essence of the previous shape of the wheat, will remain unchanged. Put simply, no other plant can grow from a wheat seed but wheat, and all wheat plants will always go through the same growth pattern from the moment they sprout to the moment they shrivel.

Similarly, all human children mature through the same growth sequence. This is why we can estimate when a child should start developing certain skills, and when new foods can be introduced. Without this fixed pattern, we wouldn't be able to chart the growth curve of human babies or anything else, for that matter.

3. Attributes that Change through External Forces

Even though the seed remains the same kind of seed, its appearance may change as a result of environmental influences such as sunlight, soil, fertilizers, moisture, and rain. So while the kind of plant remains wheat, its "wrapping," the attributes of the wheat's essence, can be modified through external elements.

Similarly, our moods change in the company of other people or in different situations, even though our selves (beds) remain the same. Sometimes, when the influence of the environment is prolonged, it can change not only our mood, but even our character. It's not the environment that creates new traits in us; it's just that the company of some people activates certain aspects of our nature more than others.

4. Changes in the External Environment

The environment that affects the seed is in itself affected by other external factors, such as climate, air quality, and nearby plants. This is why we grow plants in greenhouses and artificially fertilize their soil. We try to create the best environment for plants to grow.

In our human society, we constantly change our environment. We advertise new products, elect governments, attend schools of all kinds, and spend time with friends. Therefore, to control our own growth, we should learn to control the kinds of people we spend time with, and especially the people we look up to. Those are the people who will influence us the most.

If we wish to become corrected—altruistic—we need to know which social changes will promote correction, and follow them through. With this last factor—the changes in the external environment—we shape our essence, change our bed's attributes, and consequently determine our fate. *This is where we have freedom of choice.*

CHOOSING THE RIGHT ENVIRONMENT FOR CORRECTION

Even though we cannot determine the attributes of our bed, we can still affect our lives and our destinies by choosing our social environments. In other words, because the environment affects the attributes of the bed, we can determine our own futures by creating an environment that will promote the goals we want to achieve.

Once I have chosen my direction and built an environment to steer me there, I can use society as a booster to accelerate my progress. If, for example, I want money, I can surround myself with others who want it, talk about it, and work hard to get it. This will inspire me to work hard for it as well, and turn my mind into a factory of money-making schemes.

And here's another example. If I am overweight and I want to change that, the easiest way to do it is to surround myself with people who think, talk, and encourage each other to lose weight. Actually, I can do more than surround myself with people to create an environment; I can reinforce the influence of that environment with books, films, and magazine articles. Any means that increases and supports my desire to lose weight will do. I will still have to watch my diet, but the emotional effort required to do it—the main obstacle in any diet—will be significantly reduced, if not eliminated.

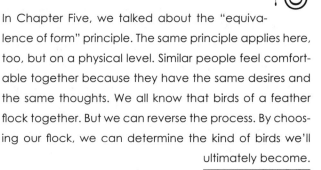

Birds of a Feather

In Chapter Five, we talked about the "equivalence of form" principle. The same principle applies here, too, but on a physical level. Similar people feel comfortable together because they have the same desires and the same thoughts. We all know that birds of a feather flock together. But we can reverse the process. By choosing our flock, we can determine the kind of birds we'll ultimately become.

It's all in the environment. AA, drug rehabilitation institutions, Weight Watchers, all of these use the power of society to help people when they cannot help themselves. If we use our environments correctly, we can achieve things we would never even dare to dream. And best of all, we wouldn't feel that we were making any effort to achieve them.

The desire for spirituality is no exception. If I want spirituality and I want to increase my desire for it, I need only have the right friends, books, and films around me. Human nature will do the rest. If a group of people decides to become like the Creator, nothing can stand in their way, not even the Creator Himself. Kabbalists call it, "My sons defeated Me."

So why aren't we seeing a "spirituality rush?" Well, there's a little hitch: *you can't feel spirituality until you already have it.* The problem is that without seeing or feeling the goal, it's very hard to really want it, and we already know that it's very hard to accomplish anything without a great desire for it.

Think of it this way: everything we want in our world is a result of some external influence on us. If I like pizza, it's because friends, parents, TV, or another source told me how good it is. If I want to be a lawyer, it's because society gave me the impression that being a lawyer somehow pays off.

But where in our society can I find something or someone to tell me that being similar to the Creator is great? Moreover, if no such desire exists in society, how did it suddenly appear in me? Did it pop up out of the blue?

Not out of the blue; out of the *Reshimot*. It's a memory of the future.

Way back in Chapter Four, we said that *Reshimot* are records, memories that have been registered within us when we were higher up on the spirituality ladder. These *Reshimot* lie in our subconscious and emerge one by one, each evoking new or stronger desires from past states. Moreover, because *all of us* were once higher up on the spiritual ladder, we will *all* feel the awakening of the desire to go back to those spiritual states when it is our time to do so. This is why *Reshimot* are memories of our own future states.

Therefore, the question shouldn't be, "Why do I have a desire for something the environment didn't introduce to me?" Instead, we should ask, "Once I have this desire, how do I make the most of it?" And the answer is simple: Treat it as you would treat anything else you want to achieve—think about it, talk about it, hear others talking about it, read about it, and do everything you can to make it important. When you do this, your progress will accelerate proportionally.

In The Mishnah (*Avot*, 6:10) there is an inspiring (and true) story of a wise man by the name of Rabbi Yosi Ben Kisma, the greatest Kabbalist of his time. One day, a rich merchant from another town approached him and offered to relocate the rabbi to his own town. He wanted the rabbi to open a seminary for the town's wisdom-thirsty people. The merchant explained that there were no local sages in his town, and that the town was in need of spiritual teachers. Needless to say, he promised Rabbi Yosi that all his personal and educational needs would be met with first-class treatment.

To the merchant's great surprise, Rabbi Yosi declined resolutely, stating that under no circumstances would he move to a place where there were no sages. The dismayed merchant tried to argue and suggested that Rabbi Yosi was the greatest sage of the generation and that he didn't need to learn from anyone.

"In addition," said the merchant, "by moving to our town and teaching our people, you would be doing a great spiritual service, since here there are already many sages, and our town hasn't any. This would be a significant contribution to the spirituality of the whole generation. Would the great Rabbi at least consider my offer?"

To that, Rabbi Yosi replied: "Even the wisest sage will soon become unwise when dwelling among unwise people." It was not that Rabbi Yosi didn't want to help the merchant's townsmen; he simply knew that without a supportive environment, he would lose doubly—failing to enlighten his students, and losing his own spiritual degree.

NO ROOM FOR ANARCHISTS

All this talk about building the right society may lead you to think that Kabbalists are anarchists, willing to obstruct the social order to promote building spiritually oriented societies. Nothing could be further from the truth.

As Yehuda Ashlag explained very clearly, and as any sociologist or anthropologist will confirm, human beings are social creatures. In other words, we don't have a choice but to live in societies, as we are offshoots of one common soul. Thus, it is clear that we must also conform to the rules of our society and care for its wellbeing. And the only way to achieve this is if we adhere to the rules of our society.

However, Ashlag also states that in any situation that is *not* related to society, society has no right to limit or oppress the freedom of the individual. Ashlag even goes so far as to call those who do so "criminals," stating that when it concerns one's spiritual progress, Nature does not require that the individual obey the majority's will. On the contrary, spiritual growth is the personal responsibility of each and every one of us. By doing so, we are improving not only our own lives, but the lives of the whole world.

It is imperative that we understand the separation between our obligations to the society we live in and to our personal spiritual growth. Knowing where to draw the line and how to contribute to both will free us from much confusion and misconceptions about spirituality.

The rule in life should be simple and straightforward: In everyday life, obey the rule of law; in spiritual life, evolve individually. Individual freedom can only be achieved through our choices in our spiritual evolution, an area where others must not interfere.

THE EGO'S INEVITABLE DEATH

The love of liberty is the love of others; the love of power is the love of ourselves.

~William Hazlitt (1778 - 1830)

Let's take another look at the basics of Creation. The only thing that the Creator created is our will to receive, our egoism. This is our essence. If we learn how to "de-activate" our egoism, we will restore our connection with the Creator. When we act unselfishly, we will regain equivalence of form with Him as it exists in the spiritual worlds. Deactivating our egoism is the beginning of our climb up the spiritual ladder, the beginning of the correction process.

One of Nature's ironies is that people who indulge in selfish pleasures cannot be happy. There are two reasons for that:

1. Egoism is a Catch-22: if you have what you want, you no longer want it. To understand why, think of your favorite food. Now, imagine yourself in a fancy restaurant, comfortably seated at a table as the smiling waiter brings you a covered plate, places it in front of you, and removes the lid. Hmmm... that deliciously familiar scent! But the minute you start to eat, the pleasure diminishes. The fuller you become, the less you're enjoying the meal. Finally, when you are full, you can no longer enjoy the food and you stop eating. You don't stop because you're full, but because eating is no fun on a full stomach. Satisfying your desire for food has quenched the pleasure from eating it.

2. A selfish desire enjoys not only satisfying its own whims, but making others dissatisfied. To better understand this reason, we need to go back to the basics. Phase One in the Four Basic Phases wants only to receive pleasure. Phase Two is already more sophisticated, and wants to receive pleasure from giving, since giving is the Creator's state of being. If our development had stopped at Phase One, we would be satisfied the minute our desires were fulfilled and wouldn't care what others possessed.

However, Phase Two—the desire to give—compels us to notice others so we can give to them. But because our basic desire is to receive, all we see when we look at others is that "they have all kinds of things that I don't." Because of Phase Two, we will always compare ourselves to others, and because of Phase One's will to receive, we always want to be better than them. This is why we take pleasure in others' deficiencies.

The second reason is also why the poverty line changes from country to country. According to Webster's Dictionary, the poverty line is "a level of personal or family income below which one is classified as poor according to governmental standards." Thus, by definition, poverty and lack are relative, not absolute.

If everyone around me were as poor as I am, I wouldn't feel poor. But if everyone around me were wealthy, and I only had an average income, which in the west is more than enough to live on, I'd still feel like the poorest person on Earth. In other words, our norms are dictated by the combination of Phase One (what we want to have) and Phase Two (comparing ourselves to others).

As it happens, Phase Two, our desire to give, which should have been the guarantee that our world would be a good place to live in, is actually the reason for all the evil in this world. This is the essence of our corruption. The desire to give is not enough, replacing the intention to receive with an intention to give is what we need to correct. This is what will make us similar to the Creator.

THE CURE

No desire or quality is naturally evil; it's how we use it that makes it so. Ancient Kabbalists have said: "Envy, lust, and (the pursuit of) honor bring a man out of the world," meaning out of our world and into the spiritual world.

How so? We've already seen that envy leads to competitiveness, and competitiveness generates progress. But envy has far greater consequences than technological or other worldly benefits. In the "Introduction to The Book of Zohar," Baal HaSulam writes that humans can sense others, and therefore want what others have. As a result, they are filled with envy and want everything that others have, and the more people have, the emptier they feel. In the end, they want to devour the whole world.

Eventually, envy makes us settle for nothing less than the Creator Himself. But here Nature's humor plays a trick on us once more: The Creator is a desire to give, altruism. Although we are initially unaware of it, by wanting to be Creators, we are actually craving to become altruists. Thus, through envy—the ego's most treacherous and harmful trait—our egoism puts itself to death, just as cancer destroys its host organism until it, too, dies along with its host.

Once again we can see the importance of building the right social environment. If we are forced to be jealous, we should at least be *constructively* jealous (jealous of something that will bring us to correction).

Kabbalists describe egoism like this: Egoism is like a man with a sword that has a drop of enchantingly luscious, but lethal potion at its tip. The man knows that the potion is a venomous poison, but he cannot help himself. He opens his mouth, brings the tip of the sword to his tongue, and swallows...

A just and happy society cannot rely on monitored or "channeled" selfishness. We can try to restrain egoism through rule of law, but this will work only until circumstances toughen, as we've seen with Germany—a democracy until it democratically elected Adolf Hitler.

We can also try to channel egoism to benefit society, but that has already been tried with Russia's communism, and failed miserably.

Even America, the land of freedom of opportunity and capitalism is failing to make its citizens happy. According to the New England Journal of Medicine, "Annually, more than 46 million Americans, ages 15-54, suffer from depressive episodes." And the Archives of General Psychiatry announced: "The use of potent antipsychotic drugs to treat children and adolescents... increased more than fivefold between 1993 and 2002," as published on the June 6, 2006 edition of the *New York Times*.

In conclusion, as long as egoism has the upper hand, society will always be unjust and will disappoint its own members one way or another. Eventually, all egoism-based societies will exhaust themselves along with the egoism that created them. For everyone's benefit, we just have to make it happen as quickly and as easily as possible.

FAKE FREEDOM

Kabbalists relate to our inability to sense the Creator as "concealment of the Creator's face." This concealment creates an illusion of freedom to choose between our world and the Creator's (spiritual) world. If we could see the Creator, if we could really sense the benefits of altruism, we would undoubtedly prefer His world to ours.

His world is a world of giving and of pleasure, but because we do *not* see the Creator, we do not follow His rules. Instead, we constantly break them. In fact, even if we did know the Creator's rules but could not see the pain we bring ourselves by breaking them, we would probably still break them. Why? Because of our belief that life is much more enjoyable as an egoist.

Baruch Ashlag, Yehuda Ashlag's son and a great Kabbalist in his own right, wrote down in a notebook words he'd heard from his father. The notebook was later published under the title, *Shamati (I Heard)*. In one of his notes, he wrote that if we were created by an Upper Force, why don't we feel this Force? Why is It hidden? If we knew what It wanted of us, we wouldn't be making mistakes and we wouldn't be tormented by punishment.

How simple and joyous would life have been if the Creator had been revealed! We wouldn't doubt His existence and we could recognize His guidance over us and over the whole world. We would know the reason for our creation, see His reactions to our actions, communicate with Him, and ask for His counsel before every act. How beautiful and simple life would be!

Ashlag ends his thoughts with the inevitable conclusion: Our one aspiration in life should be to reveal the Creator.

In Chapter Six, we said that the whole of Nature obeys only one law: The Law of Pleasure and Pain. In other words, everything we do, think, and plan is designed to either increase our pleasure or decrease our pain. We have no freedom in that. But because we are unaware that we are governed by these forces, we *think* we are free.

However, to be truly free we must first be liberated from the reins of the pleasure-and-pain law. And because our egos dictate what is pleasurable and what is painful, we find that to be free, we must first be freed from our egos.

CONCEALMENT—A REQUISITE FOR FREE CHOICE

Ironically, true freedom of choice is possible only if the Creator is concealed. This is because if one option seems preferable, our egoism leaves us no choice but to go for it. In that case, even if we choose to give, we'll be giving in order to receive—egoistic giving. For an act to be truly altruistic and spiritual, its benefits must be hidden from us.

If we keep in mind that the whole purpose of Creation is to eventually be liberated from egoism, our actions will always be heading us in the right direction—towards the Creator. Therefore, if we have two choices and don't know which of them would bring us more pleasure (or less pain), then we have a real opportunity to make a free choice.

If the ego does not see a preferable choice, we can choose according to a different set of values. For example, we could ask ourselves not "what action would produce more fun for us," but instead ponder "what would be more giving?" If giving is something we value, this will be easy to do.

We can either be egoists or altruists, either thinking of ourselves or thinking of others. There are no other options. Freedom of choice is possible when both options are clearly visible and equally appealing (or unappealing). If I can only see one option, I will have to follow it. Therefore, to choose freely, I have to be aware of my own nature and the Creator's nature. A truly free choice means that I don't know which will be more pleasurable; only in this way can I neutralize my ego.

IMPLEMENTING FREE CHOICE

The first principle in spiritual work is "faith above reason." So before we talk about implementing free choice, we must explain the Kabbalistic meanings of "faith" and "reason."

FAITH

In just about every religion and belief system on Earth, faith is used as a means to compensate for what we cannot see or clearly perceive. In other words, because we cannot see God, we have to *believe* that He exists. In this case, we use faith to compensate for our inability to see God. This is called "blind faith."

But faith is used as compensation not just in religion, but in practically everything we do. How do we know, for example, that the Earth is round? Did we ever fly to outer space to check it out for ourselves? We believe the scientists who tell us that it's round because we think of scientists as reliable people we can trust when they say that they checked it out. We believe them; it's faith.

But it is blind faith. Wherever and whenever we cannot see for ourselves, we use faith to complete the missing pieces of the picture. But this is not solid information—it is blind faith.

In Kabbalah, faith means the exact opposite of what we just described. Faith, in Kabbalah, is a tangible, vivid, complete, unbreakable, and irrefutable perception of the Creator, Nature—life's rule of law. Therefore, the only way to acquire faith in the Creator is to become exactly like Him. Otherwise, how will we know beyond a shadow of a doubt exactly who He is, or that He even exists?

REASON

Webster's Dictionary offers two definitions for the term, "reason." The first definition is "cause," but it's the second definition that interests us. Reason, according to Webster's, has three meanings:

1) The power of comprehending, inferring or thinking, especially in orderly rational ways;
2) Proper exercise of the mind;
3) The sum of the intellectual powers.

As synonyms, Webster's offers these options (among others): intelligence, mind, and logic.

Now let's read some of the insightful words Kabbalist Baruch Ashlag wrote in a letter to a student, explaining Creation's "chain of command." This will clarify why we need to go *above* reason.

"The will to receive was created because the purpose of Creation was to do good to His creatures, and for this purpose there must be a vessel to receive pleasure. After all, it is impossible to feel pleasure if there is no need for the pleasure, because without a need, no pleasure is felt.

This will to receive is the whole man (Adam) that the Creator created. When we say that man will be imparted eternal delight, we refer to the will to receive, which will receive all the pleasure that the Creator planned to give it.

The will to receive has been given servants to serve it. Through them, we will receive pleasure. These servants are the hands, the legs, the sight, the hearing, etc. All of them are considered one's servants. In other words, the will to receive is the master and the organs are its servants.

And as it usually happens, the servants have a butler among them who watches over the master's servants, ensuring that they work for the desired purpose of bringing pleasure, as this is what the master—the will to receive—wants.

And if one of the servants is absent, the pleasure related to that servant will be absent, too. For example, if one is deaf, he or she will not be able to enjoy music. And if one cannot smell, one will not be able to enjoy the fragrance of perfume.

But if one's brain is missing (the supervisor of the servants), which is like the foreman who watches over the workers, the whole business will collapse and the owner will suffer losses. If one has a business with many employees but lacks a good manager, one might lose instead of profit.

However, even without the manager (reason), the boss (the will to receive) is still present. And even if the manager dies, the boss still lives. The two are unrelated."

Apparently, if we want to beat the will to receive and become altruists, we must first overcome its "chief of staff"—our very own reason! Therefore, "faith above reason" means that faith—becoming exactly like the Creator—should be above (more important than) reason—our egoism.

And the way to come by that is twofold: On the personal level, it is studying and finding a circle of friends that will help create a social environment that will promote spiritual values. On the collective level, it requires that society as a whole learns to appreciate altruistic values.

APPENDIXES

Appendix One
Frequently Asked Questions

WHAT IS THE WISDOM OF KABBALAH?

What is Kabbalah?

Kabbalah is not theoretical research. It is a practical method intended to help us through every moment of our lives. Through Kabbalah, one discovers the future, the past, one's attributes when he or she first descended into this world many lifetimes ago, and the distance one still needs to traverse.

Seeing "both ends of the rope," Kabbalists understand what to do to benefit their lives and ours, and how best to do it. Kabbalists can also see the forces operating on them at any given moment in time, such as why one should marry a specific individual, or why one's children behave as they do.

What is the wisdom of Kabbalah about?

The wisdom of Kabbalah encompasses the entire reality below the Creator: the worlds, everything within them, the descent of the soul into this world, and its return upwards. In other words, the wisdom of Kabbalah contains all of humanity's states and situations.

All the worlds, including ours, stand one below the other. The Light emerges from the Creator and traverses all the worlds down to this world. Therefore, each element that is present in the world *Adam Kadmon* is also present in all the other worlds. Kabbalists define this relationship as "root and branch."

In his essay, "The Essence of the Wisdom of Kabbalah," Baal HaSulam defines the root and branch connection in the following way: "Thus, there is not an item of reality or an occurrence of reality found in a lower world that you will not find its likeness in the world above it, as identical as two drops in a pond, and they are called 'Root and Branch.' That means that that item, found in the lower world, is considered a branch of its pattern in the higher world, which is the root of the lower item, as this is where that item in the lower world was imprinted and made to be."

We therefore see that every element and detail in this world, with all its connections, is also present in all the Upper Worlds, from *Assiya* to *Adam Kadmon*.

The universe, Planet Earth, the still, vegetative, animate, and the speaking are all found in the worlds above this world, too. There is only one difference between the elements of this world and the elements of the Upper World: in the Upper Worlds, the elements are forces, and in our world, they are matter.

Using Kabbalah, we can attain the Upper Worlds and discover the forces that operate upon every item in this world. When we attain this level, we come to know the modes of behavior of every element of that world's reality, its qualities, and the reason for its behavior. The wisdom of Kabbalah facilitates our ascension to the Upper World and permits us to observe every object's behavior in our world from above.

What is the source of the name, *The Book of Zohar?*

Zohar means "radiance," as it is written in *The Book of Zohar*: "The righteous sit with their crowns on their heads, and delight in the splendor of Divinity." According to *The Book of Zohar*, the sensation of the Creator (the Light) is called "Divinity." In any place where the books of Kabbalah say, "so it was written in the book..." they always refer to *The Book of Zohar*. All other books are seemingly not considered "books" because the word, "book," (*Sefer* in Hebrew) comes from the word *Sefira*, which comes from the word "sapphire," radiance, a revelation (of the Light, the Creator). And this is found only in *The Book of Zohar*.

Some people suffer their entire lives ... why is this so and why is there suffering at all?

Everyone suffers all the time. Humanity in general has been suffering throughout its history. People lived and died without ever understanding the actual reasons for their pain. The pain should accumulate and reach a certain level before we can discover the reasons for it, and who or what is responsible for it.

The wisdom of Kabbalah is a method that addresses the question of humanity's suffering and how it can be resolved. As a whole, humankind has already accumulated enough pain to begin to ask about the reasons for it. In fact, this is why Kabbalists are now opening the wisdom of Kabbalah to everyone.

WHAT IS SPIRITUALITY?

How do you discern between corporeal and spiritual?

Spiritual is that which is absolutely not "for me," but only "for the Creator," when the outcome of the act is not related in any way to the one who performs it, even indirectly.

What is the "point in the heart," and do we all have it?

Every person has a point in the heart, but many people still don't feel it because they haven't "matured" or ripened enough to feel it. During our life cycles, we come to a situation where the point in the heart is revealed. In that state, we begin to feel a desire for spirituality, for the Upper One. This is called "the point in the heart."

What is the difference between this world and the spiritual world?

This world is the lowest point that a Kabbalist attains. It is the total opposite of the Creator and is termed, "the exile in Egypt." The natural power that works on us in this state, the power of our egoistic nature, doesn't allow us to do anything if it isn't for ourselves. This state is called "the state of Pharaoh."

Our egoism doesn't let us feel the sublime, perfect state. It is egoism, man's inner and vicious force called "Pharaoh," that the Torah (Pentateuch) speaks of at length. The force that liberates us from that state and admits us into the spiritual world is called "Moses." Pharaoh, Moses, and everything that is written about the Exodus describe spiritual states and emotions that we all experience at some point in our spiritual growth.

THE REVELATION OF THE CREATOR

Does the Creator exist?

The Kabbalah is studied precisely in order to feel and see the Creator. Everyone will discover and experience Him. Only when we discover the Creator will we be truly able to say that He exists, because then we will know for ourselves.

Discovering the Creator is only possible according to the measure of equivalence of qualities with the Creator. If we could feel the Creator right now, we would be Kabbalists.

If Pharaoh had priests capable of doing what Moses did and even more, how can I know that the Creator is better than Pharaoh?

There is only one power: the Creator. He influences us in a variety of ways, using contradicting forces. In this way, He forms us, affecting us in various ways, generating diverse reactions. As a result, we develop an attitude toward the Light and toward the darkness, and we will ultimately understand the meaning of giving and receiving.

The created desire in its entirety, which is equal to the Creator's greatness, is called "Pharaoh." When one is born, one receives only a small desire, and little by little discovers one's inner Pharaoh. And to the extent that one can overcome Pharaoh, so does one ascend in spirituality.

The difference between the Creator and Pharaoh is not in their power, but in their goal. If it is "for myself," it is Pharaoh; if it is for the Creator, it is the end of correction.

What is love?

Love is a consequence of equivalence of inner traits, meaning attributes. In Kabbalah, there is only one law: "the law of equivalence of form, attributes and desires." If two spiritual objects are equal in their attributes, they unite. That does not mean that from two they have now become one, but rather, that they are *as* one. Everything that happens to one of them is immediately experienced in, and enriches, the other.

"Love" is that mutual sensation that two separate objects share between them, when there is absolute equality between them (be it two people, or the Creator and a person). Love is the sensation of equivalence of spiritual attributes. Remoteness of attributes and desires distances people from one another, even to the extent of hate.

Affinity of desires, thoughts and attributes (which is actually the same, because the attributes determine the thoughts and the desires), makes them draw near, love and understand one another. When one achieves that similarity of attributes with the Creator, one also discovers the Creator and loves Him. Kabbalah states that the greatest pleasure in the world is the sensation of equivalence of form with the Creator.

KABBALAH IS NOT MYSTICISM

How does Kabbalah explain supernatural phenomena such as healing or out-of-body travels?

Kabbalah enables you to live in the spiritual world and in this world simultaneously. It helps you to feel, see, and understand your spiritual growth. By studying it, you will learn to see your past, present, and future, and you will know how to lead your life more wisely.

Supernatural phenomena are not spiritual. They are natural, physiological phenomena of which people remote from Nature are simply unaware. Kabbalah, however, speaks of a spiritual body, about what happens with the soul. In other words, Kabbalah speaks of one's transformation from egoism to altruism—the nature of the Creator.

Which charm is the best for success in life?

Kabbalah is a science with clear and concise laws that must be studied. It has nothing to do with charms, blessings, or other items or rituals done in its name. The misconceptions regarding Kabbalah originate from the time Kabbalah was concealed from people and ascribed magical forces. The books of Kabbalah clearly explain what steps we need to take to acquire true spiritual knowledge. With the knowledge you acquire, you will know which action is best for you in any given situation.

There are many methods and teachings to achieve spirituality. Why choose Kabbalah?

The difference between other teachings and Kabbalah, as I understand it from the perspective of the Kabbalah, is that they are built on the nullification of desires, or at least on suppressing them. Kabbalah, however, states that the Creator can be sensed precisely by expressing the desire for Him, only by inverting the aim of its use, and certainly not by nullifying it. He can *not* be sensed by nullifying the desire to discover Him.

Is Kabbalah a mystical experience?

Kabbalah is not a mystical experience. It is an explanation of a system of natural laws of which we are all part, and which we must learn to use to our benefit. These laws are active on all levels of Nature—still, vegetative, animate, and speaking. Therefore, when we discover them, we can improve all aspects of our world, from climate change to social structures.

STUDYING KABBALAH

Does studying Kabbalah mean I must retire from daily life?

There is no requirement to fast or to mortify yourself. One does not have to leave everyday life or abandon family duties. Nor does one float in the air or practice breathing exercises in order to attain tranquility.

Quite the contrary, students build their egos and turn them into vessels that *help* them attain their sublime goal—to sense the Creator. To study Kabbalah and understand how the Upper World operates, one must be at the center of that world and act from within it.

Therefore, one must continue doing all his or her mundane duties. The attainment of the spiritual reality must be in one's corporeal senses, and closely connected with one's normal life.

Where and how is freedom of choice expressed? When exactly does one choose, and what should one choose?

The choices that we have during our lives are narrowed down to our discovery of what compels us to study Kabbalah. Besides the study of Kabbalah, all other pursuits are considered "animate," since they are transitory and expire when the physical body dies. As human beings, we have freedom of choice only in our decision to study Kabbalah. There are three reasons that compel us to study Kabbalah:

1. Reward and punishment in this world;
2. Reward and punishment in the next world;
3. Bestowal upon the Creator, when we are driven by the desire to resemble Creator's attribute of bestowal.

We study Kabbalah as a means to attain the ultimate altruistic goal: to bestow upon Him who created us.

For these three reasons, spirituality is higher than us. We cannot convince our bodies to give to the Creator because our bodies immediately retaliate with the question, "What will I get out of it?" By its very nature, the body (which in Kabbalah is defined as "the will to receive") cannot understand bestowal.

Thus, we have no choice but to ask the Creator to give us the desire and the will to bestow, to act and to think regardless of if and how this will benefit us. If we focus all our thoughts and desires on attaining that trait, the Creator will replace our corporeal nature with a spiritual one.

Then, in contrast to when we could not understand the possibility of working for others, now we cannot understand *not* working for the Creator.

When I try to read *The Book of Zohar*, I find it very difficult to understand. Is it just me or is it truly a very difficult book to grasp?

The Book of Zohar is a very important Kabbalistic book, but it is written in a concealed way, making it impossible to understand until a person is in the spiritual world. Because of that, it is suggested that we do not begin to study straight from *The Book of Zohar*. Instead, there are introductions and books by Baal HaSulam that teach us how to understand what is written in *The Zohar*.

The Book of Zohar is not a book through which one can attain spirituality; it was written for those who have already attained it. To understand it properly, we first need to study several other texts, such as "Preface to The Wisdom of Kabbalah," "Introduction to The Book of Zohar," "Preface to The Book of Zohar," and "Foreword to The Book of Zohar." Without first acquiring clear and correct knowledge through those introductions, the book will remain completely abstruse to us.

Lately, there have begun to appear various study groups for Kabbalah. Is it worthwhile to check them out?

It is always worthwhile to explore, at least once, who studies and how they study Kabbalah. It will also help you get to know yourself. Therefore, I advise you to check things out and decide if it will be right for you.

Is there a difference in how men and women study Kabbalah?

Both men and women must develop spiritually, and the only difference between them lies in the method. The beginning of the learning process is the same. That is why our introductory courses feature the same method for men and for women. Later on, if a person goes deeper into the study of the actual Kabbalah, the difference in the method becomes apparent. Men and women will begin to sense the world differently, because men and women are indeed two different worlds and have a different perception of creation.

What do Kabbalists mean by "attainment"?

In Kabbalah, understanding the Thought of Creation—the deepest level of understanding—is called "attainment." Put differently, attainment is the ultimate degree of understanding. Attainment of a state (or degree) means that you perceive every single element in that state.

What is a prayer?

The feelings in our hearts are prayers. But the most powerful prayer, as Baal HaSulam writes, is the feeling in one's heart during study, the yearning to understand the material, meaning to match one's properties to what one is learning about.

Since everything is determined Above, where is there freedom of choice?

Man's only freedom is in the choice of environment, the society that affects us. You can read about it in Baal

HaSulam's essay, "The Freedom." Everyone's path is completely predetermined. The only way to go is forward, meaning up, to the Creator. We should want to do it ourselves, consciously; but if we don't, Nature will force us to want to progress.

If the Creator made Creation in order to delight His creations, why does He deny us pleasure?

It is not the Creator who denies us the pleasure. The reason we suffer is because of our oppositeness from Him. He is absolute goodness, and when we want to be like that, too, we will see that all He does is impart to us abundance and pleasures. But as long as we are opposite from Him, we cannot receive those pleasures because we are detached from Him.

Who can study this wisdom?

When Rav Kook was asked who was permitted to study Kabbalah, he replied: "Anyone who wants to." If a person really wants to study, it is a sign that he or she is ready.

BODY, SOUL, AND REINCARNATION

Does the Creator have a body?

Not only does the Creator not have a body, but we, too, Creation, do not have a body. A creature is not a corporeal, physical, biological body, but a pure desire to be filled with the Light of the Creator. This desire exists in each of us, and it is that which Kabbalists call "a soul."

The soul is divided into parts named after parts of the body. However, there is no connection between those parts, and the parts of the soul that are called by names of organs of our corporeal body. Kabbalists have simply found a way to express concepts in the spiritual world using words from this world. They do that by taking words of this world and using them to depict spiritual powers, which are the roots, the origins of those objects. These powers could not be expressed except through the language of roots and branches.

What does it mean to disseminate Kabbalah?

Humanity acquires knowledge about itself and the world by researching itself and its surroundings.

We create fantasies for anything we cannot understand, but wish to. These are based on analogy, speculation, and calculated conjectures grounded in whatever we already know. But however hard we try, we cannot speculate or imagine a part of the universe we have never felt. Analogy will not help either, since our senses have never experienced anything similar.

Kabbalah creates, or more accurately develops, a new sense in us. Only by developing this sense does one begin to feel *that* world. Only then is it clear that no fantasy could possibly help us perceive it.

One cannot convey such feelings to others who lack this sense. If one does possess this sense, another can pass along spiritual sensations, but only to the extent that the recipient has developed this sense.

Hence, on the one hand, Kabbalah is a science because we develop a sense of the surrounding space and research it using a strictly scientific method. On the other hand, Kabbalah differs from all other natural methods, as it is impossible to research that world without first acquiring the special sense for it. Only to the extent that one feels that world, does one begin to feel and perceive things differently.

One who doesn't feel it is unable to imagine it. The meaning and the goal of "disseminating Kabbalah" is to bring all people to feel the need to develop their souls and experience the spiritual worlds for themselves. Disseminating Kabbalah gives us a method for such a development, and teaches us how to use this newfound sense. That is why Kabbalah is a special science and not a religion.

It is written in the *Haggada* (the text read on Passover night) that Pharaoh made Israel come nearer to the Creator. How can such a negative force work for the Creator and against itself?

Pharaoh *is* the force of the Creator. It is a good force that takes a negative appearance in us, as it is written, "Two angels lead one to the goal—the 'good' and the 'bad.'"

The whole experience of progress in Kabbalah pertains to acquiring new forces of bestowal. If we had only good inclinations, we would never be able to advance. Pharaoh, the evil inclination, allows us to take from it greater desires for pleasure, correct them and thus rise even higher.

Therefore, it is important to relate to Pharaoh as a Force of the Creator that was sent to assist us. Pharaoh promotes us by evoking a desire in our egos to advance and develop materially. As a result, we gradually understand that material progress will not give us anything, and that true development is spiritual.

When, under the influence of Pharaoh, we begin to develop spiritually, we search in the spiritual world for a vessel to be filled with the desire for pleasure. Thus, our own egoism, Pharaoh, is the motivating force behind everything. This is because we cannot receive the Upper Light in our will to receive without our intention to bestow, to be like the Creator.

Instead, we can only enjoy the (very small) pleasures of our world that, once gone, leave us feeling emptier and even more dissatisfied than before.

Pharaoh motivates us to spirituality so that afterwards, when we receive the spiritual delight, he will take it for himself. In our world, Pharaoh motivates us to receive pleasure using our regular desire to please ourselves.

In the Passover *Haggada*, this is called the "old Pharaoh." Afterwards, it is said that a new king rose in Egypt. It is this Pharaoh who takes us to spirituality, and then takes it for himself.

Science has already succeeded in cloning the biological body; what about the soul?

The soul has no connection with our corporeal body. Our physical body can exist as a biological, "animate" body, with an enlivening force called the "animate soul." But that has nothing to do with the Upper Soul.

We do not ask ourselves why there are cows, chickens, or cats, or what kind of soul dwells in them. Yet they, too, have souls, but theirs are simply the animate force that sustains them, the same force that sustains our own bodies.

Therefore, a body can be cloned and there is no problem with that. In the future, all organs, and eventually an entire body will be cloned. But the soul does not depend on the body because man receives a soul according to well-defined spiritual laws, on which physical and biological sciences have no bearing. This is why we cannot clone a soul.

There are many people in our world whose Upper Soul does not exist at all. That soul is called the "point in the heart." There are people who have it, and there are those who still don't. Incidentally, we cannot know who has it and who does not.

How does a soul transfer itself into the collective soul of Adam?

The soul never actually left the collective soul; it simply stopped feeling it once it acquired an egotistical desire. But in the process of desiring correction, the soul corrects this lack of perception and rediscovers its true state in the collective soul.

Retrieving this feeling is called "the ascent up the steps of the spiritual ladder," from our world into the world *Atzilut*.

How is the individual soul separated from the collective soul?

As the soul acquires additional, uncorrected egotistical desires, it loses its sense of the spiritual world, which the soul interprets as a separation from the collective soul. As a result, it starts to feel a more crude desire in itself, called a "body." The soul feels this as "birth" in the biological body.

How does a soul get into a body?

If you mean the biological body, then the soul has nothing to do with it. But if by "body" you mean "desire, then if the desire is egoistic, it is called "a body of this world." If the desire is altruistic, it is called "a spiritual body." All these questions are explained in the "Introduction to the Book of Zohar."

APPENDIX TWO
FURTHER READING

Now that you have finished *Kabbalah for Beginners*, you must be wondering what's next. This appendix will help you decide.

We have divided the books into four categories—Beginners, Intermediate, Advanced, and All Around. The first three categories are divided by the level of prior knowledge readers are required to have. The fourth category, All Around, includes books that you can always enjoy, whether you are a complete novice or well versed in Kabbalah.

If *Kabbalah for Beginners* is your first book published by Laitman Kabbalah Publishers or Upper Light Publishing, we recommend that you read one more book for beginners, but with a different perspective, such as

Kabbalah, Science and the Meaning of Life or *From Chaos to Harmony* before you move on to the intermediate level.

BEGINNERS

Kabbalah Revealed

This is a clearly written, reader-friendly guide to making sense of the surrounding world. Each of its six chapters focuses on a different aspect of the wisdom of Kabbalah, illuminating the teachings and explaining them using various examples from our day-to-day lives.

The first three chapters in *Kabbalah Revealed* explain why the world is in a state of crisis, how our growing desires promote progress as well as alienation, and why the biggest deterrent to achieving positive change is rooted in our own spirits. Chapters Four through Six offer a prescription for positive change. In these chapters, we learn how we can use our spirits to build a personally peaceful life in harmony with all of Creation.

Wondrous Wisdom

This book offers an initial course on Kabbalah. Like all the books presented here, *Wondrous Wisdom* is based solely on authentic teachings passed down from Kabbalist teacher to student over thousands of years. At the heart of the book is a sequence of lessons revealing the nature of Kabbalah's wisdom and explaining how to attain it. For every person questioning "Who am I really?" and "Why am I on this planet?" this book is a must.

Awakening to Kabbalah

A distinctive, personal, and awe-filled introduction to an ancient wisdom tradition. In this book, Rav Laitman offers a deeper understanding of the fundamental teachings of Kabbalah, and how you can use its wisdom to clarify your relationship with others and the world around you.

Using language both scientific and poetic, he probes the most profound questions of spirituality and existence. This provocative, unique guide will inspire and invigorate you to see beyond the world as it is and the limitations of your everyday life, become closer to the Creator, and reach new depths of the soul.

Kabbalah, Science, and the Meaning of Life

Science explains the mechanisms that sustain life; Kabbalah explains why life exists. In *Kabbalah, Science, and the Meaning of Life*, Rav Laitman combines science and spirituality in a captivating dialogue that reveals life's meaning.

For thousands of years Kabbalists have been writing that the world is a single entity divided into separate beings. Today the cutting-edge science of quantum physics states a very similar idea: that at the most fundamental level of matter, we are all literally one.

Science proves that reality is affected by the observer who examines it; and so does Kabbalah. But Kabbalah makes an even bolder statement: even the Creator, the Maker of reality, is within the observer. In other words, God is inside of us; He doesn't exist anywhere else. When we pass away, so does He.

These earthshaking concepts and more are eloquently introduced so that even readers new to Kabbalah or science will easily understand them. Therefore, if you're just a little curious about why you are here, what life means, and what you can do to enjoy it more, this book is for you.

From Chaos to Harmony

Many researchers and scientists agree that the ego is the reason behind the perilous state our world is in today. Laitman's groundbreaking book not only demonstrates that ego has been the basis for all suffering throughout human history, but also shows how we can turn our plight to pleasure.

The book contains a clear analysis of the human soul and its problems, and provides a "roadmap" of what we need to do to once again be happy. *From Chaos to Harmony* explains how we can rise to a new level of existence on personal, social, national, and international levels.

INTERMEDIATE

The Kabbalah Experience

The depth of the wisdom revealed in the questions and answers within this book will inspire readers to reflect and contemplate. This is not a book to race through, but rather one that should be read thoughtfully and carefully. With this approach, readers will begin to experience a growing sense of enlightenment while simply absorbing the answers to the questions every Kabbalah student asks along the way.

The Kabbalah Experience is a guide from the past to the future, revealing situations that all students of Kabbalah will experience at some point along their journeys. For those who cherish every moment in life, this book offers unparalleled insights into the timeless wisdom of Kabbalah.

The Path of Kabbalah

This unique book combines beginners' material with more advanced concepts and teachings. If you have read a book or two of Laitman's, you will find this book very easy to relate to.

While touching upon basic concepts such as perception of reality and Freedom of Choice, *The Path of Kabbalah* goes deeper and expands beyond the scope of beginners' books. The structure of the worlds, for example, is explained in greater detail here than in the "pure" beginners' books. Also described is the spiritual root of mundane matters such as the Hebrew calendar and the holidays.

ADVANCED

The Science of Kabbalah

Kabbalist and scientist Rav Michael Laitman, PhD, designed this book to introduce readers to the special language and terms of the authentic wisdom of Kabbalah. Here, Rav Laitman reveals authentic Kabbalah in a manner both rational and mature. Readers are gradually led to understand the logical design of the Universe and the life that exists in it.

The Science of Kabbalah, a revolutionary work unmatched in its clarity, depth, and appeal to the intellect, will enable readers to approach the more technical works of Baal HaSulam (Rabbi Yehuda Ashlag), such as *The Study of the Ten Sefirot* and *The Book of Zohar*. Readers of this book will enjoy the satisfying answers to the riddles of life that only authentic Kabbalah provides. Travel through the pages and prepare for an astonishing journey into the Upper Worlds.

Introduction to the Book of Zohar

This volume, along with *The Science of Kabbalah*, is a required preparation for those who wish to understand the hidden message of *The Book of Zohar*. Among the many helpful topics dealt with in this text is an introduction to the "language of roots and branches," without which the stories in *The Zohar* are mere fable and legend. *Introduction to the Book of Zohar* will provide readers with the necessary tools to understand authentic Kabbalah as it was originally meant to be, as a means to attain the Upper Worlds.

ALL AROUND

Attaining the Worlds Beyond

From the introduction to *Attaining the Worlds Beyond*: "...Not feeling well on the Jewish New Year in September 1991, my teacher called me to his bedside and handed me his notebook, saying, "Take it and learn from it." The following morning, my teacher perished in my arms, leaving me and many of his other disciples without guidance in this world.

He used to say, "I want to teach you to turn to the Creator, rather than to me, because He is the only strength, the only Source of all that exists, the only One who can really help you, and He awaits your prayers for help. When you seek help in your search for freedom from the bondage of this world, help in elevating yourself above this world, help in finding the self, and help in determining your purpose in life, you must turn to the Creator, who sends you all those aspirations in order to compel you to turn to Him."

Attaining the Worlds Beyond holds within it the content of that notebook, as well as other inspiring texts. This book reaches out to all those seekers who want to find a logical, reliable way to understand the world's phenomena. This fascinating introduction to the wisdom of Kabbalah will enlighten the mind, invigorate the heart, and move readers to the depths of their souls.

Basic Concepts in Kabbalah

This is a book to help readers cultivate an *approach to the concepts* of Kabbalah, to spiritual objects, and to spiritual terms. By reading and re-reading in this book, one develops internal observations, senses, and approaches that did not previously exist within. These newly acquired observations are like sensors that "feel" the space around us that is hidden from our ordinary senses.

Hence, *Basic Concepts in Kabbalah* is intended to foster the contemplation of spiritual terms. Once we are integrated with these terms, we can begin to see, with our inner vision, the unveiling of the spiritual structure that surrounds us, almost as if a mist has been lifted.

Again, this book is not aimed at the study of facts. Instead, it is a book for those who wish to awaken the deepest and subtlest sensations they can possess.

APPENDIX THREE
ABOUT BNEI BARUCH

Bnei Baruch is a group of Kabbalists in Israel, sharing the wisdom of Kabbalah with the entire world. Study materials in over 20 languages are based on authentic Kabbalah texts that were passed down from generation to generation.

HISTORY AND ORIGIN

In 1991, following the passing of his teacher, Rabbi Baruch Shalom HaLevi Ashlag (The Rabash), Rav Michael Laitman, Professor of Ontology and the Theory of Knowledge, PhD in Philosophy and Kabbalah, and MSc in Medical Bio-Cybernetics, established a Kabbalah study group called "Bnei Baruch." He called it Bnei Baruch ("Sons of Baruch") to commemorate the memory of his mentor, whose side he never left in the final twelve years of his life, from 1979 to 1991. Rav Laitman had been Ashlag's prime student and personal assistant, and is recognized as the successor to Rabash's teaching method.

The Rabash was the firstborn son and successor of Rabbi Yehuda Leib HaLevi Ashlag, the greatest Kabbalist of the 20th century. Rabbi Ashlag authored the most authoritative and comprehensive commentary on *The Book of Zohar*, titled *The Sulam Commentary (The Ladder Commentary)*. He was the first to reveal the complete method for spiritual ascent, and thus was known as Baal HaSulam ("Owner of the Ladder").

Today, Bnei Baruch bases its entire study method on the path paved by these two great spiritual leaders.

THE STUDY METHOD

The unique study method developed by Baal HaSulam and his son, the Rabash, is taught and applied on a daily basis by Bnei Baruch. This method relies on authentic Kabbalah sources such as *The Book of Zohar*, by Rabbi Shimon Bar-Yochai, *The Tree of Life*, by the Holy Ari, and *The Study of the Ten Sefirot*, by Baal HaSulam.

While the study relies on authentic Kabbalah sources, it is carried out in simple language and uses a scientific, contemporary approach. Developing this approach has made Bnei Baruch an internationally respected organization, both in Israel and in the world at large.

The unique combination of an academic study method and personal experiences broadens the students' perspective and awards them a new perception of the reality they live in. Those on the spiritual path are thus given the necessary tools to research themselves and their surrounding reality.

THE MESSAGE

Bnei Baruch is a diverse movement of many thousands of students worldwide. Students can choose their own paths and the personal intensity of their studies, according to their unique conditions and abilities. The essence of the message disseminated by Bnei Baruch is universal: "unity of the people, unity of nations and love of man."

For millennia, Kabbalists have been teaching that love of man should be the foundation of all human relations. This love prevailed in the days of Abraham, Moses, and the group of Kabbalists that they established. If we make room for these seasoned, yet contemporary values, we will discover that we possess the power to put differences aside and unite.

The wisdom of Kabbalah, hidden for millennia, has been waiting for the time when we would be sufficiently developed and ready to implement its message. Now, it is emerging as a solution that can unite diverse factions everywhere, better enabling us, as individuals and as a society, to meet today's challenges.

ACTIVITIES

Bnei Baruch was established on the premise that "only by expansion of the wisdom of Kabbalah to the public can we be awarded complete redemption" (Baal HaSulam).

Therefore, Bnei Baruch offers a variety of ways for people to explore and discover the purpose of their lives, providing careful guidance for the beginners and the advanced student alike.

Kabbalah Today

Kabbalah Today is a free monthly paper produced and disseminated by Bnei Baruch. It is apolitical, non-commercial, and written in a clear, contemporary style. Its purpose is to expose the vast body of knowledge hidden in the wisdom of Kabbalah at no cost and in a clear, engaging format and style for readers everywhere.

Kabbalah Today is distributed for free in every major U.S. city, as well as in Toronto, Canada, London, England, and Sydney, Australia. It is printed in English, Hebrew, and Russian, and is also available on the Internet, at *www.kabtoday.com*.

Additionally, a hard copy of the paper is sent to subscribers at delivery cost only.

Internet Website

Bnei Baruch's homepage, *www.kabbalah.info*, presents the authentic wisdom of Kabbalah using essays, books, and original texts. It is the largest Kabbalah website on the net, and contains a unique, extensive library for readers to thoroughly explore the wisdom of Kabbalah. Additionally, there is a media archive, *www.kabbalahmedia.info*, containing more than 5,000 media items, downloadable books, and a vast reservoir of texts, video and audio files in many languages. All of this material is available for free download.

Kabbalah Television

Bnei Baruch established a production company, ARI Films (*www.arifilms.tv*) specializing in the production of educational TV programs throughout the world, and in many languages.

In Israel, Bnei Baruch broadcasts are aired live through cable and satellite on Channel 98 Sunday through Friday. All broadcasts on these channels are free of charge. The programs are adapted specifically for beginners, and do not require prior knowledge of the material. This convenient learning process is complemented by programs featuring Rav Laitman's meetings with publicly known figures in Israel and throughout the world.

Additionally, ARI Films produces educational series and documentaries on DVDs, as well as other visual teaching aids.

Kabbalah Books

Rav Laitman writes his books in a clear, contemporary style based on the key concepts of Baal HaSulam. These books serve as a vital link between today's readers and the original texts. All of Rav Laitman's books are available for sale, as well as for free download. Rav Laitman has thus far written thirty books, translated into ten languages.

Kabbalah Lessons

As Kabbalists have been doing for centuries, Rav Laitman gives a daily lesson at the Bnei Baruch center in Israel between 3:15-6:00 a.m. Israel time. The lessons are simultaneously translated into six languages: English, Russian, Spanish, German, Italian, and Turkish. In the near future, broadcasts will also be translated into French, Greek, Polish, and Portuguese. As with everything else, the live broadcast is provided gratis to thousands of students worldwide.

Funding

Bnei Baruch is a non-profit organization for teaching and sharing the wisdom of Kabbalah. To maintain its independence and purity of intentions, Bnei Baruch is not supported, funded, or otherwise tied to any government or political organization.

Since the bulk of its activity is provided free of charge, the prime source of funding for the group's activities is donations, tithing—contributed by students on a voluntary basis—and Rav Laitman's books, which are sold at cost.

HOW TO CONTACT BNEI BARUCH

1057 Steeles Avenue West, Suite 532
Toronto, ON, M2R 3X1
Canada

194 Quentin Rd, 2nd floor
Brooklyn, New York, 11223
USA

E-mail: info@kabbalah.info
Web site: www.kabbalah.info

Toll free in USA and Canada:
1-866-LAITMAN
Fax: 1-905 886 9697